# What business leaders and coachees say about Shantha:

Shantha is one of those individuals who everyone genuinely enjoys working with.... I saw how his leadership energised people, yet he always had a sense of calm and focus to ensure delivery was achieved. I had team members often comment how much they enjoyed the opportunity to work with and learn from Shantha. His genuine passion for mentoring and coaching is evident in his interactions with the people he works with. He is someone who makes time for others. He kindly spent time with my team to share his career path and how he thinks about his career development, which they found truly valuable.

**Eve Weatherburn**
**Founder & Managing Director**
**Brand Journey**

He has always been a great role model to the teams he led as well as his peers. A passionate leader, great with coaching and mentoring future leaders for IHG.... A humble leader who is well respected and able to command the room when he speaks. Has led many successful team transformations as well as being recognized for many of his personal and team achievements. Always had a strong desire to succeed and able to put team agenda before self. Was a pleasure to work with.

**Clarence Tan**
**Former Managing Director South East Asia**
**& Korea InterContinental Hotels Group**

I have had the pleasure of knowing Shantha for over 15 years now and am privileged to have been mentored by him through these years, immensely helping me progress through my leadership journey. Shantha has been a unique leader bringing to the table a power-packed combination of integrity, strategic thinking, people leadership, execution focus and ability to consistently deliver business results. Shantha has always maintained a high level of self-awareness and added to this, his learning agility meant that he has put in a lot of effort to continuously improve himself and stay current.

Standing out amongst all his qualities are his visionary and strategic thinking skills and people leadership skills.... He has been able to bring a cohesive and inspired approach from his team to deliver each time without fail. Shantha's people leadership skills are evident in the way he is able to identify strengths of every single team member, and inspire them to do that one percent extra, complemented by his genuine and committed effort to coaching and mentoring his team.... I have had a ringside view of him bringing his vision and strategy to life through strong conviction and persistent communication, active delegation and influence, transforming careers of many colleagues in the journey.

He rounds his personality with a huge level of respect, gratitude and humility in every interaction, making him a truly authentic leader.

**Samir M C**
**Managing Director**
**Fortune Park Hotels Ltd (ITC Group)**

It was always about working together and him being on the sideline, coaching and mentoring and giving us full credit for our achievements. That is perhaps one of his best qualities…. Shantha was always setting audacious goals for himself and others. He acted as a mentor, letting me take my risks, make my mistakes and learn from there without panicking. Through the various stages of my career progression, he was always there to raise the bar, forcing me to step up my learning and deliver results I thought were not possible. His ability to spot latent talent is amazing. His adjustment of his leadership style and accuracy of asking the right question is mind boggling. In summary his coaching and mentoring capabilities are unmatched.

**J T**
**Coachee/Mentee**

He has an ability to get the best out of anyone who works with him. He is truly an inspirational leader and one learns a lot as he always has a challenge for you…. Like me, many executives have had the opportunity to be coached and led by him and have progressed really well in life. I can never forget a quote from him, "The only person that stands between you and success is YOU". Believe in yourself and you can achieve anything in life.

**A K**
**Coachee**

# BELIEVE
## Helping leaders UNLOCK their true potential

SHANTHA DE SILVA

Published by Authority Connect in 2021

Authority Connect is an imprint of OMNE Publishing

Text © Shantha de Silva 2021

All rights reserved. No part of this book may be reproduced by any mechanical, photographic, or electronic process, or in the form of a phonographic recording; nor may it be stored in a retrieval system, transmitted or otherwise be copied for public or private use — other than for "fair use" as brief quotations embodied in articles and reviews — without prior written permission of the publisher.

Paperback ISBN 9780648848622
Hardcover ISBN 9780648848646
Kindle ISBN 9780648848639

Any opinions expressed in this book are exclusively those of the author and are not necessarily the views held or endorsed by the publisher or others quoted throughout. All the information, exercises and concepts contained within this publication are intended for general information only. The author does not take any responsibility for any choices that any individual or organisation may make with this information in the business, personal, financial, familial, or other areas of life based on the choice to use this information. If any individual or organisation does wish to implement the steps discussed herein it is recommended that they obtain their own independent advice specific for their circumstances.

Hardcover printing by Gunaratne Offset (Pvt) Ltd., Sri Lanka

Print, Cover and Kindle design by OMNE Publishing

This book is available in paperback, hardcover and ebook formats.

# DEDICATION

"The past is your lesson.
The present is your gift.
The future is your motivation."
– Zig Ziglar

I would never be what I am today if not:

For the great values that I learnt from my loving parents
who taught me the greatest *lessons* in life not by word, but by deed;

For the *gift* of love from my amazing wife Renu,
who has inspired me to reach for great heights,
and encouraged me when I faced challenges;

For the *motivation* from my sons Ashan and Shanil
who have inspired me to be the best I can.

# Contents

Acknowledgements .................................................................... xi

Making the Most of this Book ............................................... xiii

BELIEVE ....................................................................................... xvii

Chapter 1: Why Believe? ............................................................. 1

Chapter 2: Are You Determined to Fail? ............................... 15

Chapter 3:   **B** — Be Real ............................................................ 29

Chapter 4:   **E** — Envision ......................................................... 41

Chapter 5:   **L** — Leverage ....................................................... 57

Chapter 6:   **I** — I, Me, Myself ................................................. 69

Chapter 7:   **E** — Explore ......................................................... 83

Chapter 8:   **V** — Validate ....................................................... 95

Chapter 9:   **E** — Enable ........................................................ 109

Chapter 10: Say Yes to No ....................................................... 121

Epilogue ...................................................................................... 133

About Shantha ......................................................................... 139

# Acknowledgements

This book would not have been possible without the help of many individuals, to whom I am very grateful.

Nivesh Bhagtani was of immense assistance to me, meticulous as usual, painstakingly reading every word and conducting research to support the theories and learnings. His continuous support throughout the process was much appreciated, but most of all, his enthusiasm was very infectious. Oomar Paurobally was a good partner in the initial stages, helping to shape the outline of the book to help make the idea come to life as best we could. I was fortunate to be able to rely on Tejas Lakhani who devoted precious time to read and review the draft of the book, providing valuable feedback. I appreciate the feedback and encouragement provided by many others.

Being a first-time author, my good friend Shehan de Silva's advice and guidance on the publishing process was invaluable in getting it off the ground. I had no idea how to set about getting it published, and his advice was of enormous help to me. The beautiful hardcover version of the book is thanks to him and Gunaratne Offset Limited.

My search for the right editor and publisher ended quickly when I came across Andrew Akratos. He introduced me to Teresa Goudie whom he holds in high regard as an editor. Teresa's insights were of immense value to me as a first-time author, and in fact shaped some of the content, ensuring that the best was brought out for your benefit.

Working with Andrew was helpful, and he was generous with the wealth of information he was eager to share. A big thank you to Teresa, Andrew and the OMNE Group, who create incredible books, for their assistance in turning my ambition into an amazing book too.

# Making the Most of this Book

You made an investment when you purchased this book, so how can you get the best return for it?

This book is the result of my desire to help people like you, leaders and aspiring leaders, to unlock your true potential by believing in yourself and avoiding the mistakes I made throughout my career. To help you do that, I have developed the BELIEVE model which encapsulates experiences I gained throughout my career and the lessons I learnt from some great leaders. My own leadership journey transformed me from a boy to a man; it took me from managing just myself to leading a team of over 8000; and from earning just five dollars a month to managing an annual revenue of nearly one billion Australian dollars. I felt that it would be rather selfish of me to keep the secrets of my success to myself, and thus the concept of this book was born.

## What's in it for me?

I am sure you must be familiar with the term, 'What's in it for me?' This question subconsciously drives almost every decision we make; from the time we wake up, to the time we switch off the lights and go to bed. Having a greater awareness of the benefits can help us make conscious decisions. That's why each of the steps of the BELIEVE model outlined in Chapters 3-9 includes a 'What's in it for me?' section, the purpose of which is to illustrate the benefits that can be derived from putting into practice the principles I share. It is designed to explore how and why it should work for you. To make the most of each step, reflect on the key messages that you are taking away, what they mean to you, and how you can apply them in your life and leadership journey.

## So what? What now?

Each step also includes a 'So what? What now?' section designed to inspire you to think of the gaps (if any) that might come to mind when reflecting on that step. Think about the questions that are prompted and what conclusions you can draw from them. Then consider your next steps and how you will apply the learnings in order to make the most of this book.

## Making it count

You can select one area of focus at a time, or a few if you feel you can balance your priorities and work on it to achieve your desired outcome, to help you unlock your true potential as a leader.

I have developed coaching programmes for leaders using the BELIEVE model to guide them in applying the learnings in their day-to-day leadership journey. I use these in my coaching sessions with leaders and potential leaders, many of whom have found them to be of great benefit. (If you are interested to learn more, please visit my website: www.shanthadesilva.com)

I have been asked to explain the purpose of this book several times. Each time, I responded in the blink of an eye that this book was all about helping leaders and aspiring leaders unlock their true potential. I was immediately challenged with the very pertinent question, "If they are leaders, wouldn't they have unlocked their potential already?" Then came the moment of truth — it was about helping leaders unlock their TRUE potential. Granted, to become a leader you need to have potential, but that does not mean that's all you need. Leaders continue to grow, continue to improve and, more importantly, their potential continues to grow. Unless they continuously develop and unlock their true potential, their leadership journeys can become stagnant and, needless to say, very frustrating.

In a 2008 Harvard Business Review article titled 'Reaching Your Potential', Robert Steven Kaplan states:

Ambitious professionals often spend a substantial amount of time thinking about strategies that will help them achieve greater levels of success. They strive for a more impressive job title, higher compensation, and responsibility for more sizable revenues, profits, and numbers of employees. Their definitions of success are often heavily influenced by family, friends, and colleagues.

Yet many ultimately find that, despite their efforts and accomplishments, they lack a true sense of professional satisfaction and fulfillment.... If you are experiencing similar feelings of frustration or even regret about the direction of your career... [you need to] examine the question, "Am I reaching my potential?" This is not the same as asking, "How do I rise to the top?" or "How can I be successful in my career?" Rather, it's about taking a very personal look at how *you* define success in your heart of hearts and then finding *your* path to get there.[1]

---
1 https://hbr.org/2008/07/reaching-your-potential

This book will help you unlock your true potential as a leader through the steps of the BELIEVE model, helping you chart the path to your defined success.

*The only person that stands between you and success is YOU.*

BELIEVE

"You must never confuse faith that you will prevail in the end — which you can never afford to lose — with the discipline to confront the most brutal facts of your current reality, whatever they might be."

- James Stockdale

## Your guide to unlocking your true potential

Have you ever seen elephants that were controlled by just a short length of rope? Did you notice that there weren't any strong chains to hold them? Did you ever wonder why?

When elephants are very young, a length of rope is used to tie them. At that stage, since the elephants are still small, the rope is strong enough to constrain them. However much they try to break free, the rope is too strong for them to do so. After trying in vain for some time, they get conditioned to the fact that there is no way they can break free. As they grow up, because they have been conditioned from a young age, they still believe they cannot break away. So much so, that they don't even try.

What is the rope that is holding you back? Do you believe in yourself? In your true potential? Or have you given up and surrendered yourself to the rope that is holding you back?

One of my all-time favourite books is 'Good to Great' by Jim Collins, in which he explores why some companies make the leap and others don't. Based on extensive research, he introduces seven characteristics of 'Good to Great' companies. While I have used all the learnings from his book and applied these seven characteristics to achieve successful business outcomes time and time again throughout my career, there is one that remains a true favourite of mine; one that is my 'go to' principle when faced with a difficult situation; one that has never failed me.

Admiral James Stockdale was the highest-ranking US Naval officer ever to be held prisoner of war in Vietnam at the infamous 'Hanoi Hilton' for over seven and a half years. In conversations with Collins for the book, Stockdale said that in all that time, he never doubted that he would get out of prison. Not only was he sure he would be freed, but he believed that he would turn the experience into a positive, defining event of his life. This concept of balancing realism and optimism when facing a difficult situation as key to achieving success was one popularised by Collins as the 'Stockdale Paradox':

> Retain faith that you will prevail in the end, regardless of the difficulties AND at the same time confront the most brutal facts of your current reality, whatever they might be.[2]

We can often find some of the greatest bits of wisdom in a paradox. Sometimes, when you first hear a paradox, it comes across as contradictory and not easy to grasp. The best way to understand a paradox is through experience, so don't be surprised if it takes some grappling before you fully grasp it. I struggled with the concept behind the Stockdale Paradox initially, but I had the perseverance to put in the hard yards to fully comprehend it, so I could use it effectively as a

---

2 Collins, J.C. (2001). *Good to Great: Why Some Companies Make the Leap… and Others Don't*. HarperCollins, p. 86.

leader, and am glad I did! My leadership story may have been very different had I not done so.

The BELIEVE model takes inspiration from the Stockdale Paradox, and I refer to it repeatedly throughout the model. If you have not done so already, it is never too late to define what success means to you, then take concrete steps towards realising it by unlocking your true potential as a leader. The BELIEVE model will serve as your guide.

> In a discussion with Collins for his book, Stockdale speaks about how the optimists fared in camp:
>
> "Who didn't make it out?"
>
> "Oh, that's easy," he said. "The optimists."
>
> "The optimists? I don't understand," I said....
>
> "The optimists. Oh, they were the ones who said, 'We're going to be out by Christmas.' And Christmas would come, and Christmas would go. Then they'd say, 'We're going to be out by Easter.' And Easter would come, and Easter would go. And then Thanksgiving, and then it would be Christmas again. And they died of a broken heart," he said.
>
> (https://bit.ly/3mztlzz)

# BELIEVE

## BE REAL
Do you understand your current reality?

## ENVISION
What would success look like for you?

## LEVERAGE
What is it that you are able to leverage to your advantage?

## I, ME, MYSELF
What gets in your way?

## EXPLORE
How best can you get there?

## VALIDATE
What are your commitments and next steps?

## ENABLE
"Impossible is nothing"

# CHAPTER 1
# WHY BELIEVE?

"For every one thing you can't do, there are 10,000 things you can."

- Dylan Alcott

# From five dollars to a billion dollars. If I can, why can't you?

The Acres of Diamonds story 'a true one' is told of an African farmer who heard tales about other farmers who had made millions by discovering diamond mines. These tales so excited the farmer that he could hardly wait to sell his farm and go prospecting for diamonds himself. He sold the farm and spent the rest of his life wandering the African continent searching unsuccessfully for the gleaming gems that brought such high prices on the markets of the world. Finally, worn out and in a fit of despondency, he threw himself into a river and drowned.

Meanwhile, the man who had bought his farm happened to be crossing the small stream on the property one day, when suddenly there was a bright flash of blue and red light from the stream bottom. He bent down and picked up a stone. It was a good-sized stone, and admiring it, he brought it home and put it on his fireplace mantel as an interesting curiosity.

Several weeks later a visitor picked up the stone, looked closely at it, hefted it in his hand, and nearly fainted. He asked the farmer if he knew what he'd found. When the farmer said, no, that he thought it was a piece of crystal, the visitor told him he had found one of the largest diamonds ever discovered. The farmer had trouble believing that. He told the man that his creek was full of such stones, not all as large as the one on the mantel but sprinkled generously throughout the creek bottom.

The farm the first farmer had sold, so that he might find a diamond mine, turned out to be one of the most productive diamond mines on the entire African continent. The first farmer had owned, free and clear... acres of diamonds. But he had sold them for practically nothing, in order to look for them elsewhere. The moral is clear: If the first farmer had only taken the time to study and prepare himself to learn what diamonds looked like in their rough state, and to thoroughly explore the property he had before looking elsewhere, all of his wildest dreams would have come true.

The thing about this story that has so profoundly affected millions of people is the idea that each of us is, at this very moment, standing in the middle of our own acres of diamonds. If we had only had the wisdom and patience to intelligently and effectively explore the work in which we're now engaged, to explore ourselves, we would most likely find the riches we seek, whether they be financial or intangible or both.

Before you go running off to what you think are greener pastures, make sure that your own is not just as green or perhaps even greener.[3]

---

[3] https://www.nightingale.com/articles/acres-of-diamonds/

Have you ever envied someone? Thought that someone else was doing better than you? That the grass was greener on the other side? If you have, then think again. Did it ever strike you that it might be because they were taking better care of what they have? On the other hand, did you consider that while you were busy looking at other greener pastures, others were looking enviously at what you had, and considered yours to be the greener pasture?

As human beings, we have a tendency to look in the mirror at ourselves and not appreciate what we have as much as we need to, while at the same time looking out of the window at others, envious of the things we don't have. Little do we realise this is a reversible cycle. As Oprah Winfrey said, "If you look at what you have in your life, you'll always have more. If you look at what you don't have in life, you'll never have enough."

## The bigger picture

I am quite the optimist; I am known to see opportunities in many situations that others normally would not. But I am mindful to always regulate this with a decent amount of reality, to ensure that I remain well-grounded at the same time. However, the reality has never hindered me in my pursuits — because I accept it, then start doing something about it. I am a firm believer that every one of us has an innate ability to do better, to improve ourselves, to be more than what we are, to make a meaningful contribution to the world and at the same time to realise our dreams. So, what holds us back?

President John F. Kennedy was visiting NASA headquarters for the first time in 1961. While touring the facility, he introduced himself to a janitor who was mopping the floor and asked him what he did at NASA. "I'm helping put a man on the moon!" he replied. The janitor got it. He understood the vision, his part in it, and he had purpose.[4] Do you understand your vision? Are you driven by a purpose, a higher purpose than the mundane that confronts you day-in-day-out? As author Simon Sinek says, "People don't buy what you do; they buy why you do it. And what you do simply proves what you believe."

So often we are busy spending time on the crowded dance floor, we forget to go up to the balcony to take in a higher-level view of ourselves and our surroundings. We can't see the forest for the trees, as the saying goes. Picture yourself being on the dance floor for a moment. What can you see? How much can you see? Is your vision relatively restricted? Being on the dance floor, we may only be seeing the few people surrounding us. We only see at eye level, and our vision can be easily hampered. We are likely to be engrossed in our immediate surroundings without the opportunity to see or appreciate the bigger picture. Now picture yourself up on the balcony looking down at the dance floor. What do you see? Is it very different? Does this change your views and thoughts of what was going on when you were on the dance floor?

It is as important for us to be in the moment as it is for us to not forget our vision, our purpose — the bigger picture. We cannot do one at the expense of the other. As with everything, there has to be a good balance of both, otherwise the quality of the outcomes may not be optimal. We have become skilled at thinking that we have a balanced view of our long-term objectives as well as our immediate

---

4 https://www.beqom.com/blog/jfk-and-the-janitor

actions. But how many of us actually spend quality time defining and refining our purpose? Do we create a purpose, and put it away only to gather dust? Or do we keep reviewing and refining it so that it does not get outdated in the dynamic and rapidly changing environment in which we live?

> There are not many corporate blunders as staggering as Kodak's strategic failure to adopt digital technology early on, which ultimately destroyed its film-based business model. Steven Sasson, the Kodak engineer credited with inventing the first digital camera in 1975, said that the reaction of the management to his invention was that it was cute, and that it should not be shared with anyone else. Rather than prepare for disruption – a time when digital photography would eventually replace film – Kodak stubbornly chose to continue to focus on improving the quality of its film. And the irony is this: George Eastman, the founder of Kodak, had twice before *avoided* similar mistakes when he retired profitable business models to embrace and capitalise on disruption, moving from dry-plate to film, and then from black and white to colour film, which was demonstrably inferior at the time.

## The new NOT normal

This rapidly changing environment has brought upon us many challenges and catastrophes over the years, but nothing prepared us for the magnitude of COVID-19 that turned the world on its head. This challenged just about everyone and everything and has changed the way we think, act and behave. VUCA (Volatility, Uncertainty, Complexity and Ambiguity) seems to have become the new norm, our new way of life. We can't know for sure what tomorrow holds, but one thing that we *can* be certain of is that it will be different to yesterday. So, what can we do today to help us still be relevant not only tomorrow, but also for the days after that?

I had the opportunity to attend a live virtual event by Jim Collins who shared his thoughts on what makes great companies succeed in uncertain times. Something he said in that session jolted me to reality — that there will never be a new normal, it will be yet another NOT normal. Think about it — isn't that the reality we face? In anything we do, adaptability is going to be key to success. If we keep doing things the way we have always done, we may not even get the same results we did in the past.

If you have a dream, a goal, a vision, do yourself a favour: Invest some time in yourself and explore further how you can make it a reality. The secret to your success is you!

## From humble beginnings

I was the youngest in a middle-class family of four children. My father, the late Rev. Dr. Lynn A. de Silva, was an author, theologian, philosopher and priest. Not only was he, and three of my uncles, priests (or ministers, as they were called in the Methodist Church in Sri Lanka), but my grandfather was also a priest. As none of my cousins showed any inclination to enter priesthood and because I was the youngest of my generation on my father's side, expectations of me were quite high. It seems I was on the path to fulfill my so-called destiny to be a priest, as I was quite an active member of the Church and the youth fellowship. My interest in my father's work went beyond the Church itself however, extending to comparative religion, a field in which he was internationally recognised for his pioneering work in Buddhist-Christian studies.

And then it happened — my hopes and dreams came crashing down when my father suddenly died of a heart attack. Ironically, it happened at the Church while attending a seminar they had organised. At the time I was still a teenager, just a few months away from my school-leaving examination. My grief was compounded by the fact that my mother, around whom my life pretty much revolved, had succumbed to cancer just over a year earlier, soon after I had completed my middle school examination. Though my mother's passing was a hard blow to absorb, I had time to prepare for the eventuality as she went through treatment for a couple of months prior. As a result of her death, I resolved to not only survive that setback but to strive to make my mother proud of me by living up to her expectations, no matter what. In hindsight, was that my first foray into the Stockdale Paradox?

But my father's death so soon afterwards was more than I could cope with at that stage, as a young vulnerable teenager.

And soon, under such trying circumstances, I had choices to make; choices that would define my entire future and would have a lasting impact on my life. If I followed the path of priesthood, I had an established platform on which to build and would continue in somewhat familiar territory. Many of my father's contemporaries would have been at hand to encourage, guide and mentor me through my journey. From a scholarly perspective, I had access to everything I needed and more in my father's library. My father once asked me if I had the intention to become a priest. My plan was to study theology, and once I completed my studies, I would evaluate how I could best use my knowledge to fulfil a higher calling, a larger purpose. And this was without fully knowing the significance of this kind of thinking, which dawned on me much later in life. After listening to my loved ones who were very supportive and gave me good advice and guidance, and after giving it much thought myself, I decided the single most important thing at that time was to quickly become as independent as possible. So, I decided not to accept the generous offer of my uncle Jayi who lived in London. He encouraged me to pursue my studies, but I didn't want to be dependent on my family for four more years. His offer still stood many years later, which I gratefully accepted, and it helped me to launch my career and embark upon the journey to where I am today.

Though I didn't realise it at the time, that was one of my earliest disruptions in life that would become a common recurrence, and a factor that would be a big influence on my career. I felt like I was the lump of clay in the hands of the proverbial potter, and I was being moulded and remoulded time and time again. My shape and form were repeatedly destroyed only to be moulded into a new shape which in hindsight, almost always turned out better. At the time it was happening, however, the painful experience of being mashed and moulded did not feel very pleasant.

After I graduated from school, I started job-searching and remember that after applying for just two jobs, I received my first invitation for an interview. It was for a role as a trainee at the Hotel Ceylon InterContinental in Colombo, one of two five-star international hotels in the whole of Sri Lanka at the time. I had no idea how a hotel operated, let alone a five-star international one. I don't know whether it was naiveté or bravado, but when they offered me the role, I accepted it. I believed in myself, and that's how my professional journey began. It has been an amazing journey that I could never have imagined as a young, orphaned teenager just out of school, and one that I would never trade for anything else, challenges and all.

## Amazing career

My journey in the hospitality industry began with InterContinental Hotels — which later became part of IHG (InterContinental Hotels Group) — one of the largest hospitality companies in the world. I went from earning just five dollars (in today's money) — not for an hour, nor a week, but for a month — to being responsible for a regional business unit generating an annual turnover of nearly AUD 1 billion. I went from working in one hotel, to running over 100 hotels, both in operation and in development, across many brands from economy to luxury. And from being responsible for just myself to leading a team of over 8000 great individuals, a cohort I grew to love, spread across many countries, cultures and continents.

So, what's the secret? I didn't know the answer to that question at the time but looking back over my long and successful career, I know it now. Throughout my professional life, I had the privilege to work with great leaders who guided me, exceptional teams that supported me, and awesome people who believed in me. The wonderful friendships and relationships built over time will always remain close to my heart and I know they have, and will continue to, enrich my life. Knowing what helped me to have an amazing career, achieve some seemingly impossible results, gain wide recognition and more importantly gain the trust and respect of many, is information I do not want to keep to myself. I would like to share my learnings with as many people as possible, in the hope that it will inspire some, including you.

The secret to my success? Belief in myself. I could never have imagined that backing myself to venture into totally unknown territory at such a young and tender age would result in the amazing heights I experienced throughout my career. I had faith in myself, albeit unaware of the full gravity of it at the time. I accepted the brutal reality I faced, because to me, what other choice did I have? But I never wavered in my faith that I could and would succeed, no matter what. I used to always say that the most important principle that guided me in my life was to *believe in God and do the right thing*. And now that I look back, I add a third element to that — to *believe in myself!*

## All because I believed

I know that if I could go from humble beginnings to have a remarkable and successful career, you can too. That is why I want to share my learnings and the secrets of my success with you. My father had a huge influence on me from a very young age — seeing his literary adventures inspired me to follow in his footsteps as an author, to write a book myself one day. After I took early retirement from my long career at IHG, I took my self-belief to an even higher level to craft an entirely new chapter of my life. Once again, I ventured into entirely unknown territory — allowing myself to be remoulded like clay yet again — and as a result the idea of writing a book became a more tangible reality. As I contemplated the best method to share my learnings and inspire others, I did not favour the idea of writing an autobiography. I felt that it would be more self-serving than serving others. My purpose was to inspire others, to help them to be better leaders. The moment I put this front and centre of my focus it quietly dawned on me — why not share some of the great stories that have inspired me (and many others) and some learnings from my experience and that of others, in a way that is easy to leverage and unlock true leadership potential.

However, I still struggled to find the best format to deliver this.

As I looked to start writing a new chapter in my life, I wanted to enrich myself with more and new knowledge by attending many courses and workshops. As a result, I attended a workshop on being an entrepreneur, conducted by Jane Jackson, a well-respected career coach and best-selling author. Being the extremely generous person she naturally is, one of the many experiences Jane shared with us at the workshop was how she developed a mnemonic based on her area of specialisation — CAREER. A lightbulb immediately lit up in my head and transposed me to a place where I was oblivious to what was going on (thankfully Jane did not pick up on that!), and I was inspired to develop my own mnemonic, right then and there, in the middle of that workshop. And thus, the mnemonic BELIEVE was born, hand-written on my iPad in light blue, along with three abstract words in red that described what it would deliver: POWER, PASSION, YOU.

And then it all came together: I was inspired to further develop the BELIEVE model in order to enable leaders to unlock their true potential. And then of course I was able to structure the contents of this book in a way that will not only be an interesting read with a wealth of information and inspirational stories, but also as a guide to leaders who want to do something more with that information, leaders who want to unlock their true potential. And I hope that leader includes you.

*I chose not to be a product of my DNA, but a product of my actions,*

*I always strived to push myself beyond the norm, challenging the proverbial 'glass ceiling',*

*I demanded a lot from myself as I did from others, so we can unlock our true potential — together,*

*I had great aspirations; and supported them with strong work ethics and punishing schedules,*

*I was ready to give it all, always; I knew no other way to live up to my purpose:*

**To make the world a better place by striving to be a better person, and an inspiration to others.**

*All because I believed.*

# CHAPTER 2
# Are You Determined to Fail?

"Failure is so important. We speak about success all the time. It is the ability to resist failure or use failure that often leads to greater success. I've met people who don't want to try for fear of failing."

- J.K. Rowling

## Failures are signposts on the road to success

I have faced failure, repeatedly. Then it dawned on me: My failures were merely signposts on the road to my success. Imagine you are a basketball player for a moment. How would you feel if you were entrusted with taking the winning shot in a basketball game, everyone's hopes were pinned on you, and you missed? Not once. Not twice. 26 times! What if you missed thousands of shots? What if you lost nearly 300 games? What if you failed over and over and over again? What thoughts would go through your mind if you were in this situation? How would it make you feel?

Let's take another journey, this time moving away from sports to the world of entrepreneurship. Imagine you had the opportunity to start a magazine, and you were excited because this gave you the opportunity to interview many prominent personalities. And then, as a true entrepreneur, you capitalised on an opportunity to expand — to leverage the magazine to sell records at a discounted rate. Because this was so successful, you opened a shop selling records but, after enjoying early success, something went wrong. You made a mistake, one that would cost you dearly. You inadvertently labelled the records as export stock, resulting in hefty fines and unpaid taxes. You didn't have the means to pay them, so your mother came to your rescue. She re-mortgaged her house to help you pay the dues. What thoughts would go through your mind if you were in this situation? How would it make you feel?

I was fortunate enough to work with some leaders who not only gave me great opportunities, but also second chances. Time and time again I took on roles and responsibilities that were way beyond my 'perceived' ability because I had strong self-belief. I took on roles in countries and locations that were not the most favoured destinations for many, without hesitation. I chose to work with a wide range of leaders who had very different styles of leadership. I once took on a role and immediately received calls from concerned colleagues who warned me of the predicament my predecessors faced — two of whom left the business. Still, I backed myself and believed that things would not be the same for me — and sure enough they turned out to be quite different! One of the highlights of my career was when I took on a role that polarised many people. Some thought I was out of my mind to take on such a role that had 'loser' written all over it. Yet some others, who believed in me a little bit more, thought it was one of the best things that could have happened to me. My family and I left behind very comfortable lifestyles and moved from much sought-after locations for less appealing ones time and time again. Did I have a choice? Yes, I did, and I exercised that choice — to back my words with actions — and to back my belief that I could and would succeed. Despite inheriting seemingly less-successful situations, I used that and leveraged it into a journey of success. In the eyes of the world (well not all, just some) I may have been repeatedly viewed as a loser, but that didn't deter me; it only helped make my resolve to succeed even stronger.

Going back to the two stories above, could you have guessed that the first one is what Michael Jordan shared about his experiences? Yes, that was Michael Jordan! I can't imagine anyone who has not experienced some sort of failure in their career or in their life. I have, and quite frankly not once, not twice, but many times over, and I have no doubt that you have too. And you will continue to do so. But what differentiates the successful from the failures? As Winston Churchill aptly said, "Success is stumbling from failure to failure with no loss of enthusiasm."

> From the NBA History website:
>
> By acclamation, Michael Jordan is the greatest basketball player of all time. Although, a summary of his basketball career and influence on the game inevitably fails to do it justice, as a phenomenal athlete with a unique combination of fundamental soundness, grace, speed, power, artistry, improvisational ability and an unquenchable competitive desire, Jordan single-handedly redefined the NBA superstar. Even contemporaneous superstars recognized the unparalleled position of Jordan. Magic Johnson said, 'There's Michael Jordan and then there is the rest of us.' Larry Bird, following a playoff game where Jordan dropped 63 points on the Boston Celtics

> in just his second season, appraisal of the young player was: 'God disguised as Michael Jordan.'
>
> (https://www.nba.com/history/legends/profiles/michael-jordan)
>
> Now re-read the first paragraph of this chapter again – does it sound familiar in any way?

Take a look at the second story again. That is a description of Richard Branson's early ventures. He did not deter in the face of failure. Failure did not stop him. He is someone widely recognised for his entrepreneurial spirt, not letting anything or anyone stand in the way of realising his dream, be it a business venture or an audacious personal ambition. Once again Winston Churchill's words of wisdom come to mind: "Success is not final; failure is not fatal: it is the courage to continue that counts."

> Richard Branson, who is synonymous with his Virgin brand, struggled in school and dropped out at age 16 – a decision that ultimately led to the creation of Virgin Records. (On a side note, remember the age 16, this comes up a couple of more times. They say 'sweet 16' – maybe it really is a sweet spot!) His entrepreneurial projects started in the music industry and expanded into other sectors, including the space-tourism venture Virgin Galactic, making him a billionaire. He is also known for pulling off some great stunts: power boat racing and for the first crossing of the Atlantic Ocean by hot air balloon.

## No, but, however

So, what differentiates successful people from those who are not? Is it their capability? Is it their intelligence? Or does it lie in the opportunities they have been given? The simple answer is none of the above. The main differentiator is belief: Belief in themselves that they can make their dreams, goals, vision a reality. But what about the impact of their environment? There is a lot of talk about the 'new normal' but, as we discovered earlier, the new normal may be just a myth — there cannot be a new normal, because we live in a VUCA world. We are surrounded by volatility, uncertainty, complexity and ambiguity more so than ever before, therefore self-belief must be a constant.

Achieving success does not mean you have to do it at any cost, says one of my favourite authors, Marshall Goldsmith, in his New York Times bestselling book 'What Got You Here Won't Get You There', in which he shares 20 habits that you need to break. He says that one of the biggest mistakes that leaders make is wanting to win too much — the need to win at all costs and in all situations — and when it matters, when it doesn't, and when it's totally beside the point.

Goldsmith is not only a member of the Thinkers50 Hall of Fame and the only two-time #1 Leadership Thinker in the World; he was also ranked as the World's #1 Executive Coach and Top Ten Business Thinkers for eight years. I was privileged to listen to him in person twice within the space of a few months. Every time I listen to him, he never ceases to amaze me with his selflessness and passion to be of help to others, a lesson we all can benefit from. His mission is to help successful leaders get better. And here's one of the powerful things

I have learnt that can help you turn your failures into successes, as Goldsmith says:

> An easy habit for people who like to win to fall into, and a sure-fire shortcut to killing conversations, is to start a sentence with "no," "but," or "however". It doesn't matter how friendly your tone is or how honey sweet you say these words, the message to your recipient is "You are wrong." It's not "Let's discuss," "I'd love to hear what you think," it's unequivocally, "You are wrong and I am right." If your conversation companion is also of the winner variety, you have a potential battle on your hands, and there is nothing more that can happen that is productive.[5]

Here's a good practise for you to adopt as you set out to make the most of this book — challenge yourself to avoid starting sentences with the words "no", "but" or "however". Want to make it a bit more interesting? Set yourself a consequence every time you use one of those words — and be true to yourself! If you follow this, you will see the impact it has on the outcomes you achieve. You can even take it a step further and ask someone to check on you or keep tabs on it at home or at work to help you break the habit. For those of you who are parents, think about how often you have started a sentence with your kids, especially teenagers, with one of these three words. If you are in denial that you have this habit, observe yourself and I'm sure you will be surprised. Try starting sentences using the words "yes" or "and" instead.

---

[5] https://www.marshallgoldsmith.com/articles/no-but-however/

> In a live webinar I attended, Goldsmith talked about a billionaire and philanthropist who donated billions to charity and signed up to the Giving Pledge, an initiative that Bill Gates and Warren Buffett founded to encourage the world's wealthiest to donate half of their wealth or more to charity. A few days after he made that massive contribution, Goldsmith had a coaching session with him. Goldsmith had established a system of 'fining' his coachees $20 every time they started a sentence with one of three words: "no", "but" or "however", and he donated these 'fines' to charity. He started this system with the billionaire at his coaching session, and after a couple of 'fines' the billionaire complained that it hurt! Goldsmith reminded him of the massive donation he made a couple of days before, and that got him thinking. What difference did $20 or a couple of hundred dollars make to a man who had just donated billions? The difference, he explained, was that donating the billions of dollars was winning, and the $20 'fine' was losing – even if it was eventually donated to charity!

## Are you determined NOT to fail?

Given the circumstances we are in — and I write with full knowledge that times are bound to change — I am confident that we are likely to continue to face increased uncertainty in our lives and the leadership journeys ahead of us. In such situations we are likely to be faced with the propensity of failures — or perceived failures — more often than not. How are you going to avoid being a victim of your failures? There is a difference between failure and becoming a victim; the difference being mindset. Victims dwell on their failures and wallow in self-pity therefore find it difficult to move on. Those who don't have a victim's mindset accept that they have failed while acknowledging that they can learn from their experience to change their future. Let me share a personal experience with you, one that was probably the hardest to come to terms with, the bitterest pill I had to swallow — and believe me, I have had to swallow more than my share of bitter pills.

As I shared earlier, I have had an amazing career in hospitality. Believe it or not, it was with just one company spread over a period of nearly four decades! And then one day I finally had the dreaded conversation — the time had come to make a call on my future, and it felt like I had been hit by a bolt of lightning. To be fair, it was not entirely unexpected as, over a period of time, I had many discussions centring around my future career plans, and my intention to remain in Australia even at the expense of prematurely ending my career. It was time for me to focus more on myself, my family, and trying to integrate further into the country which we had decided to call home for the rest of our lives. So, we set a timeline, and the end was now approaching. It still felt bitter as I had been totally loyal to one company only, probably to my detriment, as all I knew was centred around that company. I made the difficult decision to end my career early with the sole organisation I had worked with (for many more years than I had spent with my wife!) and take early retirement rather than pursue other career opportunities. I loved what I was doing and enjoyed it beyond measure, and it seemed difficult to start a life outside of it. This organisation had literally been my life. Being very frank, I did wallow in self-pity for a few days, but *only* for a few days as early retirement was not the way I envisaged ending my illustrious career.

And then I resolved to rise from the ashes, so to speak. Yet again the potter was at work re-moulding the clay, and this time I had the opportunity to decide the shape and form it took. I decided to focus on the things that were most important to me and my family — probably one of the rare occasions in my life. My commitment to my work and career meant I had been separated from my family for prolonged periods of time, very often. Every single move to a new location during my career meant that I was separated from my family for at least a few months at a time. I am very blessed to have an amazing wife, Renu, who many times had to be both a mother and a father to my two boys Ashan and Shanil as they grew up. I missed being around for many family celebrations, birthdays, graduations and even the birth of my second son — whom I saw for the first time a few days after he was born. I even sat through a day of annual budget reviews despite taking time away from work so that I could attend the funeral of my brother, who had suddenly passed away 24 hours earlier.

After a long wait spanning many years, we finally moved to Australia, our chosen home; only I was never there as I was travelling overseas nearly 200 days of each year. That's when I decided it was time; time for me and my family — finally — and I have not looked back since then.

To start with, you would not be reading this book if I did not make that choice. Since I made the break, I have had some of the best times of my life. Renu and I did a trip literally around half of Australia, driving half the way, and flying the rest — that was the first thing I ticked off my bucket list. We enjoyed it so much that it even prompted me to sell my beloved car in favour of a more 'road trip-friendly' one — sparking my new love of vehicles!

Unfortunately, on the very day I retired, Renu fell and fractured her knee and had very limited mobility for nearly three months. This meant that I had to run the household including cooking, cleaning, washing and doing many more chores, things that I had avoided for most of my nearly four-decades long career. I had spent so much time away from home — I guess it was payback time! But it was also a source of great joy for me, and I enjoyed the opportunity to care for her so much. When many gained much weight due to the COVID-19 lockdown, I took on an exercise and diet regimen that saw me lose 20% of my body weight and be in the best shape I had ever been.

My early retirement gave me the opportunity to share the knowledge I had gathered over my long career through taking on consulting in hospitality. I was able to bring to life my passion to pay it forward and to share the amazing experiences, knowledge and skills I had acquired by launching my own executive coaching and leadership mentoring practice. I had the opportunity to help many people, because now I had time to focus on them. I could finally share my knowledge with a wider audience by participating in numerous panel discussions and interviews and writing for publications. I was able to expand my own knowledge by exploring areas and disciplines hitherto alien to me. And most of all, you are reading this book because I finally realised my passion to write a book and combined it with my purpose to inspire others. Who would have thought? I did. I had a vision and I rose from the ashes, bigger, better and stronger, to make it a reality. And you can too!

Are you determined NOT to fail?

I want to share with you my journey, and the mistakes I made;

I want to share with you my learnings;

I want to share with you what worked, and how it worked;

I want to share with you why it worked, and who made it work;

I want to share with you that I did it, and that you can too;

And most of all, I would love to see that you do it too!

All of us have choices to make. I made many choices in my life, many of which were made in the face of looming failure that could have resulted in dire consequences for me personally. I made choices, and you need to also. You need to choose wisely. I have 'risen from the ashes' and taken another step towards fulfilling my purpose to be an inspiration to others, by helping them to unlock their true potential. What about you?

# CHAPTER 3
# BE REAL

"Reality is that which, when you stop believing in it, doesn't go away."

- Philip K. Dick

## Do you understand your current reality?

You want answers?

*I think I'm entitled*

You want answers?

*I want the truth!*

You can't handle the truth!

Have I got your attention? Do you want the truth? Can you handle the truth?

That was a classic exchange between Jack Nicholson and Tom Cruise in the American legal drama *A Few Good Men*, when Nicholson gets riled up under skilful cross examination. I thought this would be a great introduction to what we are about to explore. We do not always want to know the truth. Maybe because at times, the truth hurts. We often prefer to have our heads in the sand and ignore the truth for as long as we possibly can. We like to do this so that we can go on our merry ways, although fully aware that it is unlikely to last forever.

Red pill or blue pill? A hacker by night, Neo was a computer programmer by day who faced a real dilemma in *The Matrix*, a must-see on any sci-fi greatest movies list. If he takes the red pill, he will become part of the human resistance and face reality. If he takes the blue pill, he will forget he ever knew the real world and live in ignorant bliss. What would you choose if you were in Neo's position? Take the blue pill and live in bliss, oblivious to reality and make the most of the short-term enjoyment while it lasts? Or would you be bold, take the red pill and come to terms with the current reality you are facing? You want to know what choice Neo made? He chose to take the red pill and guess what happened? He of course became the hero! Likewise, you can become your own hero — make use of this book to help guide you through a journey to achieve success, starting with facing your own reality.

## Facing brutal facts

Remember the Stockdale Paradox I introduced earlier? In a paradox, we often find great gems of wisdom and I am a firm believer in the Stockdale Paradox which advocates that balancing realism and optimism in a dire situation is key to success. The foundation of the Stockdale Paradox, *facing the brutal facts of the current reality,* has come to my aid time and time again throughout my career. We often move into action mode before we take stock of the current situation, with corresponding results that don't necessarily make us proud.

I attended my very first General Managers Leadership Conference in 2005 soon after becoming the GM of the Holiday Inn Park View Singapore as it was known then (it is known today as the Holiday Inn Singapore Orchard City Centre, a name I take great pride to have been instrumental in establishing, which helped us achieve much success). There are two things that stand out in my memory even to this day.

The first is when we were socialising after the gala awards dinner; my boss walked up to me and asked when I was going to receive an award — I will share the sequel to that story later. The second is that this was where a highly influential book, 'Good to Great' by Jim Collins that I mentioned earlier, was recommended to me and the first thing I did on my way back home was to grab a copy at the airport.

When I took over as the GM of the hotel in 2005, it was underperforming, much to the dissatisfaction of the stakeholders. The difficult part for me was sifting through all the feedback, comments, reasons and excuses that I received and trying to get to the bottom of things. I am glad that I had the discipline to focus and unearth the brutal facts that we were facing.

It was an ageing hotel back then. On the other hand, the hotel was in a fantastic location that we could capitalise on. Once we started peeling the onion and ultimately faced the brutal facts of our reality (and accepted them for what they were), we were able to chart a path to success resulting in an amazing turnaround, and we went from envying others to *being* the envy of others.

One small example of the success we achieved was nearly doubling the average room rate within a short span of time, without changing the product or the team. In fact, on the subject of the team, I was given a lot of 'advice' as to what changes I needed to make to the team to be successful. But once I faced the brutal facts, I was able to discard some of this 'advice' with confidence. Some of the very same team members who were thought to be unsuitable for their roles ended up becoming super stars. One thing that I hold dear to my heart to this day is this great team who truly embodied the attitude that nothing was impossible!

Sometimes, without taking the time or having the patience to get the brutal facts, we get 'trigger happy' and try to reinvent the wheel before understanding what the reality is. We all know what the outcome of such actions are likely to be. For example, when I was learning to drive, the part that I hated most was having to look over my right shoulder. We all know that there is a blind spot in the rear-view mirror that we need to watch out for, hence the necessity to look over your shoulder. Thanks to advancements in technology, many car manufacturers have come up with solutions to help drivers by incorporating a sensor into the side mirrors, which as you can guess is a favourite feature of mine. But at times it also can make us a bit complacent. Do you regularly look over your shoulder? What blind spots might you have that you are not aware of? What are you doing about finding and addressing those blind spots? What are you doing about facing the reality?

## Feedback is a gift

We all know the value of feedback. I personally like to seek and receive feedback. I use 360 feedback surveys frequently to gain insight from a wide group of people I interact with. I have a habit of asking questions like: What is missing? What could I do better? If you were in my position what would you do? When I took on a new role, I always made a point to clarify expectations from all stakeholders. Not only the bosses and the direct reports, but also those on the frontline. This way I could envision what the future looked like for each of them, which in turn helped formulate my vision and road map and gave me a great appreciation of the current reality. It often made me squirm when I received some of the feedback; it made me uncomfortable. Some of the feedback also lingered at the back of my mind for a long time, until I did something about it, or closed it out. This is one of the secrets of my success — face the brutal facts of the current reality, and then do something about it. If we don't address the current reality, it doesn't matter what we do or how much we do it, it would be like the proverbial house built without a solid foundation. And we all know how that story ends.

By the same token, I also loved to give feedback. I felt it was my obligation as a leader to help people improve and be more successful. When I say 'loved' to give feedback, I must qualify this statement. While I loved to give feedback because of the reasons I mentioned, believe me when I say it was never easy to hold a mirror in front of someone, and it took quite a bit of courage, especially initially. But as time went on, I got more confident and comfortable with it, and so did those who received my feedback. A side note — the next time you receive feedback, consider how hard it may have been for the person to deliver that feedback. Be thankful for the effort he or she has made and do something about it; it is a gift that can help you be a better leader.

Are you ready to face the brutal truths of your current reality? Confronting it is likely to be uncomfortable. But then again, if we want to grow and be successful, we need to be comfortable being uncomfortable, correct? We might fear that facing reality might lead to us having to accept our failures and shortcomings. We all have egos that we are very protective of and may be fearful that although we are open to facing reality, we might find it difficult to really come to terms with what it unearths.

I recall an incident that took place soon after I started in a new leadership role in a different country. I had barely been in my role for a month or so when I had my first one-on-one session with a senior leader. I was very forthright and upfront with this leader with my feedback. By this stage of my leadership journey, I had developed a trait of 'calling a spade a spade' even if it meant short term pain, as I knew it would bring long term gain. After the interactions with me, that leader felt it had been a 'train crash' and was bewildered to be 'hit' in the face with his current reality. In hindsight, was I brutal? If I am honest, then yes, I guess I was. But then again, I believe in being objectively honest and upfront with people. Should I have been a bit more tempered with my feedback? I really don't think so. And guess what? After the initial 'train crash', this leader went on to grow rapidly in his leadership, achieving many successes and receiving many accolades. I wonder what would have happened if as a leader I chose not to ruffle feathers and took the easy way out by permitting the status quo. I can only imagine the many sleeping giants that may have remained sleeping, maybe even to this day. The truth hurts, but it also heals.

So, what is it that you want to be better at? Are you willing to take the plunge? I can't tell you what the outcome is going to be, nor can I assure you that you are going to like it. But I know that facing your reality will help you move on to do bigger and better things, which you could not have ever dreamt of before. Just think of it as the bitter medicinal concoctions we were given as kids when we had a cough or fever. We all hated the unpleasant taste that lingered in our mouths (at least most of us did!) but we also knew that after a few doses of the bitter medicine we would feel much better.

Read what Julie Zhuo, the former vice president of product design at Facebook, now the co-founder of Inspirit and author of the book 'The Making of a Manager', has to say about becoming a manager for the first time:

> Congratulations, you're a manager! After you pop the champagne, accept the shiny new title, and step into this thrilling next chapter of your career, the truth descends like a fog: you don't really know what you're doing.[6]

She continues in the Growth Faculty blog:

> I would rather be honest about what I didn't know rather than pretend like I knew everything. It was actually a huge inflection point in my own learning, because if I could very quickly admit to someone that I was having a meeting with that I didn't understand what they were talking about or if I was sitting in a room in a presentation and honestly just didn't have the first clue of what this term was and I raised my hand and asked, it made it so much easier for me down the road and I didn't have to pretend like I was the smart person in the room.[7]

---

6 https://bit.ly/34wdGuV
7 https://www.thegrowthfaculty.com/blog/topleadershiquotesbywomen

> They say that the brutal honesty of Alan Mulally, former chief executive officer of Ford, saved the company. The story goes that when he joined Ford Motor as its new CEO in 2006, in an employee town hall, one of the first questions asked of him was what kind of car he drove. "A Lexus," he revealed to an auditorium filled with stunned Ford employees, "it's the finest car in the world." Though this was a shocking admission, it delivered a very clear message how he viewed products made by Ford. When Mulally took over the leadership, Ford was fast spiralling into a financial crisis and was desperate for a strong leader to help save it. And the result? Mulally is widely credited with turning Ford from a broken company into the industry's comeback kid!

## What's in it for me?

I hope that by now you have an appreciation for the need to face your current reality. Remember, acceptance is not equal to resignation — they are two very different things. If you are 'resigned' to something it means that you have decided there is nothing you can do about it. You have given up which will result in you feeling helpless. That is not what you want to do. The better option is acceptance which means that you accept the facts of your current reality, which in turn will help reveal your options.

As much as you will have some degree of discomfort with this initially, it will help you have a much greater appreciation of yourself, and a view of the areas that you might need to focus some attention on. This will hopefully make accepting your current reality a bit easier, now that it is out in the open, and hopefully you won't have any more 'blind spots'. This will also help minimise the fear of the unknown, of things you were scared were beyond your control. You will not see yourself as a failure but will gain much more confidence in yourself and be able to face any self-doubts.

Now that you are more confident in yourself, and feel yourself much more grounded on *terra firma*, you should be ready to explore the terrain and navigate the pitfalls that might come your way. You should realise that others also face similar issues and hopefully you won't compare yourself to them in a negative light. This will help you have a clearer mind and focus better on the things that are important for you to focus on.

And last but not least, you will see new opportunities. With your newfound awareness and enhanced confidence, you are now bound to see more of those opportunities, and you will be better positioned to capitalise on them. You will have taken the first step on your journey to realise your true potential. But more importantly, I hope this process will also make you appreciate all you already have.

## So what? What now?

A good starting point is to make a list, writing everything about your current reality that comes to mind. What is it that you are struggling with? What causes you the most stress? Pain? Anxiety? Don't restrict yourself to think just about work, think about your life. Your relationships. Everything that comes to mind, both positive and negative. If you want to explore some of the things that come up further, you can even ask a trusted friend. You don't have to, but you may find it helpful to do so.

Identify the area or areas that you want to focus on. You may want to address everything, and you can, but not at the same time. You need to prioritise and identify what is most important for you and start there. You can come back and address the others one by one, once you have progressed with the key area you have identified.

This is the foundation of the BELIEVE model and probably the toughest part of the journey to realising your true potential. The more honest and comprehensive you are at the start, the more fun the next steps will be. From facing the brutal facts of your current reality, we are going to move to a more creative and enjoyable mode, and hopefully a very exciting next step.

# CHAPTER 4
# ENVISION

"Create the highest, grandest vision possible for your life, because you become what you believe."

- Oprah Winfrey

# What would success look like for you?

Let us not wallow in the valley of despair, I say to you today, my friends. And so even though we face the difficulties of today and tomorrow, I still have a dream. It is a dream deeply rooted in the American dream. I have a dream that one day this nation will rise up and live out the true meaning of its creed: 'We hold these truths to be self-evident, that all men are created equal.'…. I have a dream today.[8]

These are words from one of the most famous moments in history, Martin Luther King, Jr.'s *I Have a Dream* speech that was delivered to over 200,000 people in 1963, which was more than any other rally previously held in Washington at that point. People took his message to heart, which included truths from the Bible and the Constitution of the United Sates. This speech almost immediately took a spot as one of the greatest in U.S. history and what Martin Luther King, Jr. was trying to achieve was to change people's minds, to share his understanding. We all know the important role his dream had in changing the world.

---

8 https://www.americanrhetoric.com/speeches/mlkihaveadream.htm

Let's continue down memory lane. Were you also guilty (unlike me, of course!) of skipping classes during school to do more 'exciting' things, like spending time with friends, or going to the movies? What is the most audacious thing you did in your childhood? Well hang on, keep it to yourself for now (maybe it is better that you keep it to yourself for the well-being of many!). How did that memory feel? Did that youthful naivete make you do things that the rational or 'wiser' you would never envision? What is the most audacious thing you would do today, given the opportunity, and if there were possibly no consequences?

## What were you doing when you were 16?

Have you ever felt strongly about something? Committed enough to support it wholeheartedly, no matter the sacrifices you would have to make? What is the one cause that you feel most strongly about now? If you were still in school, would you go to the extreme of skipping school to fight for your cause? Would you consider spending your days outside on the streets holding up a sign in the belief that your cause would have an impact on the world? Do you remember what you were doing at 16?

Let me share with you the kind of year a particular 16-year-old girl had in 2019. Not only did she become the de facto leader of a global protest movement, she delivered speeches to multiple world leaders including at the UN Climate Change Conference and World Economic Forum. She met the Pope and was nominated for the Nobel Peace Prize (twice). She was named *Time* magazine's Person of the Year, eclipsing many well-reputed world leaders (and am guessing much to the affront of some of them). She inspired 1.6 million people from 133 countries to protest the lack of action on climate change. Her achievements were much more than most of us could have ever achieved at that age — and you have probably guessed who it is: Greta Thunberg!

> On the first day of her climate strike, Thunberg was alone. She sat slumped on the ground, seeming barely bigger than her backpack. It was an unusually chilly August day. She posted about her strike on social media, and a few journalists came by to talk to her, but most of the day she was on her own. She ate her packed lunch of bean pasta with salt, and at 3 o'clock in the afternoon, when she'd normally leave school, her father picked her up and they biked home.
>
> On the second day, a stranger joined her. "That was a big step, from one to two," she recalls. "This is not about me striking; this is now us striking from school." A few days later, a handful more came. A Greenpeace activist brought vegan pad thai, which Thunberg tried for the first time. They were suddenly a group: one person refusing to accept the status quo had become two, then eight, then 40, then hundreds. Then thousands.
>
> By early September, enough people had joined Thunberg's climate strike in Stockholm that she announced she would continue every Friday until Sweden aligned with the Paris Agreement. Thus, the Fridays for Future movement was born. By the end of 2018, tens of thousands of students across Europe began skipping school on Fridays to protest their own

leaders' inaction. In January, 35,000 schoolchildren protested in Belgium following Thunberg's example. The movement struck a chord. When a Belgian environmental minister insulted the strikers, a public outcry forced her to resign.

By September 2019, the climate strikes had spread beyond northern Europe. In New York City, 250,000 reportedly marched in Battery Park and outside City Hall. In London, 100,000 swarmed the streets near Westminster Abbey, in the shadow of Big Ben. In Germany, a total of 1.4 million people took to the streets, with thousands flooding the Brandenburg Gate in Berlin and marching in nearly 600 other cities and towns across the country. From Antarctica to Papua New Guinea, from Kabul to Johannesburg, an estimated 4 million people of all ages showed up to protest. Their signs told a story.

In London: The World is Hotter than Young Leonardo DiCaprio.

In Turkey: Every Disaster Movie Starts with a Scientist Being Ignored.

In New York: The Dinosaurs Thought They Had Time, Too.

Hundreds carried images of Thunberg or painted her quotes onto poster boards. Make the World Greta Again became a rallying cry.

(Excerpt from TIME magazine's 'Person of the Year 2019' article https://time.com/person-of-the-year-2019-greta-thunberg/)

## The future is our responsibility

Bear with me for a moment as I digress to address a very important topic. Have you given much thought to climate change? What does it mean to you? Have you thought of how you contribute to it? Has it occurred to you that if not enough action is taken now, the consequences it could have not only for future generations, but even for our own generation, are dire?

The increase in global temperatures that we hear about and, in some cases experience, has devastating consequences, endangering not only the survival of plants and animals, but also the human race. A terrible impact of this phenomenon is the melting of the ice mass in the Arctic and the Antarctic regions, which in turn causes sea levels to rise. This results in flooding that threatens coastal environments, putting small island states at risk of disappearing entirely, one of which is the well-known tourist destination of the Maldives.

As a result of climate change, we also experience extreme weather conditions such as droughts, bushfires, hail and floods leading to severe adverse economic impacts and the loss of lives, livelihoods and the death of many animals. As a case in point, in the bushfires that ravaged Australia in 2019-20, an estimated three billion animals were killed or displaced. It is thought to have cost the Australian economy over four billion dollars. Mindboggling figures indeed. But that is the stark reality! I am sure many of us have experienced the effects of climate change at some point in time.

Has that moved you to think and act differently? I certainly hope it has. Even if you have not acted as yet, it is never too late to start. Every small act matters: Small drops of water ultimately make a mighty ocean. One of the simplest things you can start with is to focus on your water usage. There are so many ways that you can be more efficient — and it not only saves the planet, it saves money for you too. You can start with a small initiative such as shortening your showers by a minute or two, and collectively it can have a great impact. I have, and you can too!

## BHAGs (Big Hairy Audacious Goals)

Now let's get back to dreaming! What do you envision? What is it that you are willing to commit your time, energy and passion to? What is it that you hunger for? Greta believed in a cause and envisioned the change that was necessary to make the world a better place for future generations. In her speech to the UN COP24 climate talks in Poland where she reminded politicians of their responsibility to act for the greater good, she said, "Many people say that Sweden is just a small country, and it doesn't matter what we do, but I have learned you are never too small to make a difference."[9] Outside of Sweden, Greta was just a 16-year-old teenager no one had heard of. And today? A Google search returned over 28 million results!

So, what will it be for you? Do you want to live your life without making a greater impact for yourself, for those you love and hold dear, and the world around you? Do you want to live your life in obscurity, or do you want to live in the knowledge that you have made a difference to yourself and those around you? In the words of Greta

---

9 https://www.lifegate.com/greta-thunberg-speech-cop24

in 2019, as she addressed the annual convention of CEOs and world leaders at the World Economic Forum in Davos, Switzerland:

I want you to panic.... I want you to feel the fear I feel every day. And then I want you to act.[10]

The doubting part of you might be saying, well that was Greta, and this is me. Really? Is that what you think of yourself? If you don't believe in yourself, who else will? Yes, self-doubt will try to creep in. Yes, the nay-sayers will get to you at times. That's external, and you cannot control it. But what you can control, you should. That's the least you can do for yourself.

I vividly remember time and time again when my team members looked at me, wide-eyed, as I publicly unveiled BHAGs — Big Hairy Audacious Goals. That was a lot of fun for me, and for my team... ultimately! I felt my role as a leader was to enlighten the team about the possibilities, to inspire them to focus on the big picture, so that together we could be in a better position than if we had not done so. I can think of many examples from my career that I can share with you, too many — that is another book in itself! But let me share one such example with you now.

When I took over as the general manager of a particular hotel, we had a performance measurement system similar to a balanced scorecard that was used as a benchmark for overall hotel performance. The performance of the hotel was measured across 10 metrics, and if your team and hotel achieved all 10 of the metrics, that was the epitome of success. We were just entering the third quarter of the year,

---

10 https://bit.ly/2Lvd7uJ

we had only achieved about half of the metrics, and we were on track to achieve six or seven of our 10 metrics by the end of the year. In my inimitable style, my focus was not on achieving one or two additional metrics, I wanted the whole hog — to achieve all 10 of them! I had a great team to work with, and I believed that it was more than possible. So, we went to work on the metrics with renewed vigour and came up with a plan to achieve most of them, bar one. That was great progress, but we were faced with one seemingly insurmountable hurdle. Due to some unforeseen circumstances, we were so far behind our target that there seemed no possibility to achieve this one with any level of human effort — it called for a superhuman effort!

We HAD to do unprecedented things, a great example of a BHAG, as there was no other way. But we had a glimmer of hope, a small opportunity. We were just approaching the mid-autumn festival in Singapore, which meant that a huge number of mooncakes were purchased in celebration to share with family and friends. The hotel generated a good amount of revenue from the sale of mooncakes every year and was on track to repeat a reasonable year-on-year growth in revenue, which usually trended around a 5-10% increase. That was not going to cut it — if we were to achieve our target, we had to increase our revenue by nearly 50% over the previous year. And if we did that, it would mean that we would be able to reach the nirvana of achieving all 10 metrics.

So, in true 'Shantha-style', I challenged the team. It goes without saying, might I add, that I wholeheartedly supported them as well. I guess at first they thought I was crazy. No, they didn't say it, but I am sure that thought would have crossed the minds of some. Being the great team they were, they were unfazed in the face of this seemingly insurmountable challenge and took it head on, getting to work, thinking outside the box, and of course dreaming and envisioning. As Albert Einstein said, "The definition of insanity is doing the same thing over and over again and expecting different results." To cut a long story short, the end result was that we achieved a growth of more than 50% in revenue in a span of a few months, exceeding all expectations and setting some unprecedented sales records in the process. To borrow a term from the previous chapter, we were not resigned to the reality, we accepted the reality, and then envisioned what success looked like. And yes, we achieved the epitome of success — one of the few hotels to do so that year!

## What's in it for me?

"All men dream, but not equally. Those who dream by night in the dusty recesses of their minds wake in the day to find that it was vanity: but the dreamers of the day are dangerous men, for they may act on their dream with open eyes to make it possible."

- T.E. Lawrence;
'Lawrence of Arabia'

I will keep on dreaming and inspiring others to dream. It has made a big difference to my life as I am sure it will to yours. I must also say that dreaming and imagining is an important element of envisioning, as it influences our perception. And isn't perception what shapes our world? Our experiences depend on how we perceive things. So, by envisioning we can influence our realities. We can look at things in a more advantageous way for us. The more vivid your imagination is, the more effective you are likely to be at envisioning. A good way to imagine is to paint a picture in your mind. A detailed, vivid, colourful picture. Think about yourself in the future, in three, five or 10 years from now. Envision a time in the future and imagine that you are there. The idea is that by envisioning the future in detail, it seems more real, more likely to happen.

I used to practise this actively, even for a much shorter time frame. Since relocating to Australia, my responsibilities required me to travel a lot, so I was away more than I was home in Australia. It was a difficult situation as we had just moved and were in the midst of settling down. Don't get me wrong, I enjoyed the time I spent with the teams in the hotels, and nothing gave me greater joy during my travels than spending time with the amazing team members who brought our hotels to life, and a smile to the faces of many. But it was also very hard to leave home so often, being separated from my wife (and let me share a secret — my car!). So, every time I embarked on a trip, one of the things that kept me going was the picture I painted in my mind of returning home, and all the things I would do (and, yes, it included driving my car!).

Brian Scudamore, the founder and CEO of 1-800-GOT-JUNK? credits the success of his multi-million-dollar business on his "painted picture". Many scientific studies have found that by visualising abstract goals as pictures and videos, as Brian did, you are essentially turning your future into a story that will stick.

When I took on one of my most challenging (and in hindsight most exciting) roles as Head of South West Asia, India constituted 90% of the region and had a lot of promise, but fell short of delivering on expectations. Everyone had an opinion on India: some advocates believed in the long-term potential; and some nay sayers had very little faith. Such was the polarising impact India had. Once I went through my 'facing the brutal facts' phase and turned my attention to envisioning the success that I believed was possible, I just could not contain my excitement.

We had a great opportunity to redefine India so to speak, and more importantly I had an amazing team that was up to the task. All I had to do was to awaken the sleeping giant! Taking the lesson from John F. Kennedy's visit to NASA described earlier, I envisioned a larger purpose that would inspire the team. As leaders (including me!) at times tend to overcomplicate things, I learnt my lesson and kept it simple. Our rallying cry was "To make India #1 for IHG and IHG #1 for India". And boy did we have fun doing it. The outcome? I will share that with you later.

Have you ever taken a vacation? And if you have, did you enjoy it? I certainly hope you did — after all it was a vacation, and probably a well-deserved one too! For a moment just think about the process that took place in planning your vacation. How did you set about preparing? Did you just plan transactionally, without any emotion? Or did you dream? Imagine? Envision? Did you imagine what the experiences would be like? What the places you would stay in feel like? What the food you would eat taste like? How relaxing the spa treatment you would have feel like? And on and on. So, come to think of it, it is a very simple process. Everyone does it. Athletes do it, they envision success. Musicians do it, they even envision standing ovations. Successful business leaders do it, they envision what success looks like, what receiving that award will feel like. I have done it, and you have done it too! So now is the time to put that practice into good use. So, go ahead and start imagining, start dreaming, start envisioning. Start to paint your picture.

## So what? What now?

> KNOW VISION. KNOW SUCCESS.
> NO VISION. NO SUCCESS.

So why am I advocating envision, rather than vision? You might think that I needed to find a meaningful word to fit into my BELIEVE model — well, not really! On a more serious note, it has a deeper relevance. Let me share some insight from an interesting blog I read on Mindvalley:

By meaning, vision simply refers to the sense or ability of sight. If you can see yourself succeed, you can make that vision a reality.

So, what does envision mean then?

*Envisioning* refers to when you imagine certain events or outcomes like walk-throughs for video games, so that you can effortlessly turn them into reality.

How does that differ from visualization?

*Visualization* refers to creating visual aids that can accelerate learning, and in turn, the achievement of your goals....

Here is a list of envisioning techniques suggested by psychologists:

1. Meditating on certain positive thoughts, ideas, or methods to internalize them.
2. <u>Envisioning</u> your day in advance to avert potential threats and resolve predictable obstacles.
3. <u>Envisioning</u> the favourable outcome of an event to enable its occurrence.

In simple words the difference between vision and envision is within the technique.[11]

So, does this sound more like fun, as promised? This is an exercise that *can* be a lot of fun, but at the same time is very eye-opening too. As much as you dream, you imagine, you envision; you now need to start thinking how to make it a reality. It certainly can, and we are going to explore that in more detail next.

---

11 https://blog.mindvalley.com/envisioning

# Chapter 5
# Leverage

"When you know what you want, and you want it badly enough, you'll find a way to get it."

- Jim Rohn

## What is it that you are able to leverage to your advantage?

A 10-year-old boy decided to study Judo despite the fact that he had lost his left arm in a devastating car accident. The boy began lessons with an old Japanese Judo master. The boy was doing well, so he couldn't understand why, after three months of training the master had taught him only one move.

"Sensei," the boy finally said, "shouldn't I be learning more moves?"

"This is the only move you know, but this is the only move you'll ever need to know," the sensei replied.

Not quite understanding, but believing in his teacher, the boy kept training.

Several months later, the sensei took the boy to his first tournament. Surprising himself, the boy easily won his first two matches. The third match proved to be more difficult, but after some time, his opponent became impatient and charged; the boy deftly used his one move to win the match. Still amazed by his success, the boy was now in the finals.

This time, his opponent was bigger, stronger, and more experienced. For a while, the boy appeared to be overmatched. Concerned that the boy might get hurt, the referee called a time-out. He was about to stop the match when the sensei intervened.

"No," the sensei insisted, "let him continue."

Soon after the match resumed, his opponent made a critical mistake: he dropped his guard. Instantly, the boy used his move to pin him. The boy had won the match and the tournament. He was the champion.

On the way home, the boy and sensei reviewed every move in each and every match. Then the boy summoned the courage to ask what was really on his mind.

"Sensei, how did I win the tournament with only one move?"

"You won for two reasons," the sensei answered. "First, you've almost mastered one of the most difficult throws in all of judo. And second, the only known defence for that move is for your opponent to grab your left arm."[12]

## Appreciate what we have

We often lament about what we don't have, forgetting to appreciate what we really do have. Many times, I went down the rabbit hole desiring something that I didn't have, forgetting to be thankful for what I had been blessed with, and to make the most of it. Sometimes what we think is our biggest weakness can become our biggest strength.

---

12 https://bit.ly/3nxO9ZA

Even without knowing it, the young boy was leveraging his weakness, and just like him, that's where we can find some of our biggest strengths. While helping me review this draft, Nivesh Bhagtani, who has been a tremendous help to me in preparing this book, commented, "While trying to leverage weaknesses, we can discover our biggest strengths." How very true!

What is it that you can leverage to your advantage, to help you realise your dreams, your goals, your vision?

## Law of leverage

In his blog 'Millionaire Acts', Tyrone Solee guides others to achieve their goals, escape the rat race and become successful in life. He says:

Leverage is one of the most used words in the field of business and finance. It refers to any technique used to multiply gains. It often involves the borrowing of money from a bank to buy more assets to expand a business with the belief that the income generated from the asset bought will be more than the cost of borrowing or the interest of the loan.

The word 'leverage' came from the French word 'levier' which means to elevate or to raise, to give a minimum input that achieves maximum results, or the ability to gain more with less resources. This can be seen in the simple machines that we often use to make our lives easier, referred in science as a lever.

BELIEVE

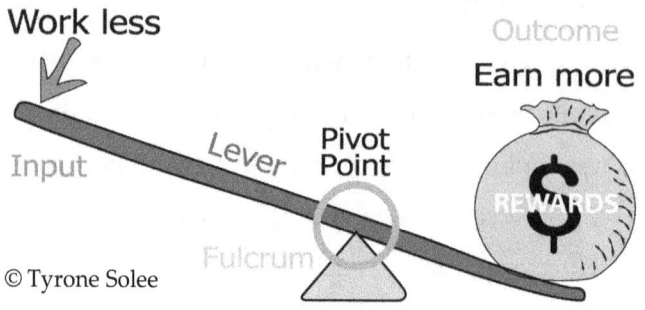

A good example is a water pump. If you have ever tried to use a manual water pump, you would have noticed that the longer the handle, the lesser effort you need to exert to fill a pail of water.

Leverage is not only applicable in business and finance, and through the use of simple machines. It encompasses almost all successful endeavours of human life; in pursuit of business alliances, in dealing with ourselves, our neighbours, and in accumulating wealth.

Take for example a real estate developer who needs someone to excavate land. For this job, he may be willing to pay 6000 dollars. There are two applicants in this job. One is willing to do manual labour with the use of a shovel so he can pocket the whole amount for himself. The other one plans to spend 1000 dollars and rent a heavy-duty digging machine.

The one who is willing to leverage the use of the machine can finish the job in one week and would be ready to accommodate another excavation job. The other person who was planning to do manual labour may or may not have finished the job even in one month and would have been very tired and exhausted at the end of it.[13]

I have often taken the term 'leverage' for granted. Once I started delving deeper into it, it opened a whole new realm of understanding for me, way beyond the simple leverage that I took for granted. Let me share my learnings with you. What comes to mind when you think of leveraging? When I think of leveraging, what comes to mind very simply put is 'more for less'. Sounds good, doesn't it?

Before I share the learnings of leveraging, it's good to first remind yourself what opportunities you have to leverage. What areas have you identified as areas that would benefit from leveraging? If you did a good job of understanding and applying the principles of 'Be Real', then you are in a good place. If not, to make the most of this I would urge you to revisit that step, ensure that you have explored your current reality to the full extent, so you can use leverage to your advantage, enabling you to enjoy the best benefits it will yield.

## More for less

Now let's explore the principles of leveraging. As I have repeatedly iterated, it is all about getting more for less. How can you get the maximum output with the minimum effort? You don't have to be shy about this. This is not about cheating or being lazy (although people may perceive it this way). It's about being smart.

One thing that changed the way I think was when I read the bestseller by Tim Ferris, 'The 4-hour Work Week'. If you have

---

[13] https://www.millionaireacts.com/3218/the-law-of-leverage.html

not read it, I recommend that you do, as it gives you much food for thought. It certainly got me thinking and changed the way I worked; for the better. One of the key takeaways from the book for me was being conscious about the cost and best use of my time. How often do we think of the time taken to do a task in terms of what it actually costs the company for you to complete that task? Have you ever stopped to consider the opportunity cost to you personally on spending time on a particular task?

My self-reflection and learnings made me a huge advocate of delegating, to a fault! On a lighter note, even though I may not have been paid that much, I could find better use of my time by delegating, which yielded a better return for the company. But I'm not talking about delegating for the sake of it. You delegate not because you are not capable, or because you are lazy, even though people might make those assumptions. Don't let that deter you. Delegating helps you achieve goals. Proper use of delegating (as opposed to abandoning — to proverbially throw a person in the deep end and let them figure out a way by themselves) can help you make better use of your time and output for your benefit and that of the organisation. It also helps motivate others by giving them the opportunity to take responsibility (and thereby accountability) that they normally would not have the opportunity to do. It can be used very effectively to develop the potential and key talents in people as it gives them exposure through the tasks that can accelerate their development. There are times when you may have too many things on your plate, and times when you just can't get going with a task, no matter how hard you try.

Take the opportunity to delegate. One of my favourite illustrations of this is that if you have 10 tasks to complete, technically you can put in 10% effort to each if you were to divide your efforts equally. Alternatively, imagine if you delegated the 10 tasks to 10 different people. How much effort can they expend for each of the tasks they are entrusted with? 100%? That means 100% effort times 10, rather than 10% effort times 10. (That is provided you do not delegate all 10 tasks to one person!) Even if they were not as capable as you are, which is likely to be better: 10% focus from you or 100% from someone else? Which is more likely to get better results? As much as I am advocating delegation, I must also remind you of some of the keys to successful delegating, such as ensuring the person has the capability for the task, has the interest and motivation to complete it (or passion), and that they receive the support they need. Delegating has much greater success when the person being given a task can see the 'WIIFM' — What's In It For Me?

In my first role as a hotel general manager, one of my successes was to leverage the strengths of the team. I had an energetic and enthusiastic team, and all I had to do was to give them the opportunity. My hotel manager thrived on responsibility and carried out most tasks better than I could have! It helped fine tune his skills under my watchful eye, resulting in him being entrusted with a general manager role in a hotel that was twice the size, and he continues to achieve much success in his illustrious career. My belief in and use of delegation certainly helped develop the team, but that was not the only positive impact. As a result of my delegating, I was able to free up time to not only think more strategically, adding value to the hotel, but also take on more responsibilities as an area general manager with the 'spare' time I generated.

Last word on delegation — to me, the golden rule is as Jim Collins says: When things go right, look out the window and shine the light on the team. And when things don't go so well, look in the mirror and take the blame. Use the opportunity to also expose your key talent to a wider audience — you owe it to them!

## What's in it for me?

Why have I spent so much time talking about delegation when we were supposed to focus on leveraging? Well, apart from the fact that you need to understand reality to make leveraging effective, you also need to be able to free up your time to focus on the areas that you need to. Delegating can be the answer to that obstacle.

So now that you have identified the areas you need to focus on, understand the principle of leveraging, and have the means to free up time to focus on the areas you need to, what do you do next?

> Early tech rivals Bill Gates (of Microsoft) and Steve Jobs (of Apple) both introduced radical innovations in the world of computing, that have had a far-reaching impact into the lives of nearly everyone on the planet. But they could not have been more different when it came to their entrepreneurial strengths.
>
> While Gates was a highly skilled software engineer who personally wrote code for Microsoft products as

> late as 1989, Jobs was an unmatched design thinker who attended calligraphy classes as an informal student, and never wrote a single line of code for Apple. These two entrepreneurs made lasting impacts with very similar product offerings, in the exact same industry, during the same period of time, but with a completely different set of strengths and skills. It was their shared ability to identify and lean on their most useful strengths & skills, that allowed them to achieve greatness. Some entrepreneurs, like Richard Branson and Mark Cuban, thrive on interpersonal skills, leveraging their people networks to grow their businesses over time. Others get their start by leveraging their well-trained technical skills, like Elon Musk and Mark Zuckerberg.
>
> (https://bit.ly/3pxeUyn)

## So what? What now?

Let's look at the various elements in the illustration I shared earlier: input, outcome, lever, and the fulcrum. Using that as an example, you should by now have an idea of what outcomes you would like to achieve as a result of your envisioning. You should also have a good appreciation of the inputs based on facing your current reality. So now what you need to do is identify which of your strengths and even weaknesses, values, beliefs or inner strengths you can use as a lever to get there, and the amount of (optimum) effort you need to expend to achieve it. Yes, don't forget your weaknesses. It may seem counterintuitive at first — why would I *want* to leverage my so-called weaknesses? Don't I want to minimise them? Mitigate them? Avoid any situations where these weaknesses may start to seep through? Like we saw in the story of the young boy, your weakness could also turn into your greatest advantage — no harm in leveraging that!

The fulcrum is "the main thing or person needed to support something or to make it work or happen" according to the Cambridge dictionary. Who or what is your fulcrum? What support do you need? Whose support do you need?

I hope you enjoyed learning more about the importance of leveraging, and the impact it can have on your success as a leader. It is a key lesson for everyone, especially leaders, because as we very well know, as much as we want to, we never have as much time as we need to do the things we would like to. So, what do we do? Could it be that leveraging is the secret to our success? That is why it is important that you spend time really understanding and identifying the best use of leverage for you. It is going to be even more pertinent in the next step when you turn the spotlight on yourself. This one's going to be very interesting to explore.

# CHAPTER 6
# I, Me, Myself

"I'm here to build something for the long-term. Anything else is a distraction."

                               - Mark Zuckerberg

"You surely don't have much faith. Why do you doubt?"

                               - Matthew 14:31

## WHAT GETS IN YOUR WAY?

Right away, Jesus made his disciples get into a boat and start back across the lake. But he stayed until he had sent the crowds away. Then he went up a mountain where he could be alone and pray. Later that evening, he was still there.

By this time the boat was a long way from the shore. It was going against the wind and was being tossed around by the waves. A little while before morning, Jesus came walking on the water toward his disciples. When they saw him, they thought he was a ghost. They were terrified and started screaming.

At once, Jesus said to them, "Don't worry! I am Jesus. Don't be afraid."

Peter replied, "Lord, if it is really you, tell me to come to you on the water."

"Come on!" Jesus said. Peter then got out of the boat and started walking on the water toward him.

But when Peter saw how strong the wind was, he was afraid and started sinking. "Save me, Lord!" he shouted.

Right away, Jesus reached out his hand. He helped Peter up and said, "You surely don't have much faith. Why do you doubt?"

Matthew 14:22-31

This is a story from the Bible that I have used many times to portray what could happen if we get distracted by what is going on around us, making us lose focus on our goal. It is a great illustration of what we are focusing on in this chapter — what gets in our way. When I read this story, it spoke volumes to me. The first message is about how self-belief forms the foundation for our abilities, achievements and possibilities. Like how Peter walked on water — because he was encouraged by Jesus and believed it was possible. The second message, which is more pertinent to what we are exploring here, is about distractions. Peter was doing well so long as his focus was on Jesus. The moment he started looking at and thinking about the raging winds, his self-belief quickly turned to self-doubt, and he began to sink. This picture remains very vivid in my memory and serves as a constant reminder of the importance of not letting anything or anyone distract me from my dreams, my goals, and my vision.

## Self-doubt

In this story, the raging winds were the cause of Peter's self-doubt and got in the way of achieving his goal. What is your raging wind? What distractions hold you back? What gets in the way of your success? If you focus on your goal diligently, no matter what, and eradicate the noise and distractions around you, that will help you get to your goal faster. It's the noise that bothers you, that slows you down, and makes you doubt yourself. That noise represents things that take your concentration away; even small things like constantly checking your email, phone or social media whilst trying to accomplish a task is a distraction. Other forms can be in comfortable habits, for example if you are someone who becomes so engrossed in spreadsheets that you lose time and focus that should have been dedicated to accomplishing other tasks. And sometimes it can be the perennial enemy: gossip.

Workplace gossip can make us distracted, derailed or even demotivated by what others say about us. The best way to overcome this challenge is by steering clear of listening to and participating in any form of gossip. Though easier said than done, that will make you stand out from the rest. The benefit? You will waste less time, have the ability to focus more on what you need to do, and as a result accomplish more. I have personally experienced this first-hand, and am sure you have too.

In my case, I had friends who got carried away with the gossip at times. Early on in my career, it bothered me a lot, and got in the way of my effectiveness and accomplishments. Worse still, gossip became rife when I was doing well in my career — why do you think that was? That in itself was an indicator of the maliciousness of gossip. Finally, I decided that I had had enough!

The most effective way to deal with this for me was to ignore what people said about me behind my back. If they didn't have the confidence to say something to my face, to share it openly, then I would seriously question the intent or the genuineness of their comments. I always liked to adopt the attitude of allowing gossip to go in one ear, and out the other. It is difficult to not let it affect you, and at times it certainly gets to you. But with time and practise, you will become more comfortable with it. There might be a nagging voice inside of you that tries hard to keep reminding you of it, sometimes even in the middle of a good night's sleep! But I am of the opinion that you cannot control what others think or say about you — so why waste your time and energy worrying about it? If by chance something that has been said has some significance or is helpful (which is very unlikely) take it on board, but that rarely happens.

What you do have influence over are the things that are in your control. Something that works as an antidote is to be the best at what you do — irrespective of the noise around you — and that will influence others' opinions, which may in turn change what they say about you. But your primary focus should not be about changing their opinions, it should be about being the best you can, and the opinion of others will be an outcome. If you focus on changing their opinions rather than letting your actions and achievements speak for you, it is likely to take you down a rabbit hole, derailing your very efforts.

If we want to realise our dreams, we need to be disciplined and focused on our goal, like a racehorse with blinkers on, an example I often use.

> **Blinkers**
>
> If you've ever watched a horserace and wondered why a number of the horses wear blinkers, then wonder no more. One of the main reasons is to make the horse stay focused on the track and limit its vision to avoid

> distractions. When a horse wears blinkers, its vision can be reduced dramatically from about 180 degrees to about 30 degrees. It is easy to appreciate therefore that unblinkered horses are more likely to be easily distracted and this is particularly dangerous in racing.

If you were to imagine having blinkers on as you focus on the task at hand, what would that mean to you? Who or what distractions would be cut away from the periphery?

We have thus far explored some elements that can get in your way: self-doubt, cutting out distractions, and keeping a sharper focus. Let me share some important leadership lessons I was fortunate to learn to help you avoid things that get in your way, things that hold you back.

I learnt many valuable leadership lessons from someone I have an immense amount of respect for — Jan Smits, former CEO of Asia, Middle East and Africa of the InterContinental Hotels Group. Amongst the many leaders who influenced my career, the person who has had the greatest impact by far is Jan and he continues to influence and support my leadership journey. I am truly privileged to have benefitted from working with him.

The first and most compelling lesson I learnt from Jan was about the importance of focusing on my self-development, on which I will elaborate further in the next chapter. The second important lesson I learnt from Jan was saying "No". When a group of us first heard Jan speak about this at a senior operations leaders meeting, we were a bit nonplussed. But gradually, the rationale dawned on us. How were we going to be successful if we kept taking on new tasks and responsibilities, and loading up to the point that we were constantly scrambling to get through our day? Now those of you who are switched on and fresh from the learnings of leveraging, I am guessing you are saying, "Delegate!" Yes, that is part of the answer. But even if you delegate, there is only so much you can take. It is absolutely amazing the impact that saying "No" has, so long as you do it the right way! People suddenly start to respect you even more. When you keep saying "Yes", you end up taking on too much, overextending yourself and inevitably failing to meet expectations. So, you need to be very selective as to what you say "Yes" to. One way to do this effectively is to focus your efforts on the areas you are good at and refer the other requests (or delegate them) to others. Ultimately, you will probably end up saying "No" more often, and that is ok. It's better to bow out respectfully than end up delivering a below-par result. As the saying goes, "less is more" as it allows you to focus on what matters.

## The third alternative

Often as humans we are conditioned to think rather selfishly: it's I, me, myself, my party, my team, my country, my child, my company, my opinion, my side against yours. Then it becomes 'me' versus 'you'. I am good, you are bad. I am right and you are wrong. In each of these situations we see two alternatives. But what if there was another option, a third alternative? That was the third important lesson I learnt from Jan. From the time I heard Jan talk about the third alternative, it changed my thinking even to this day and added an insightful new dimension to how I approached situations as a leader. I always try not to restrict myself to two-dimensional thinking, which has helped me to consider innovative ways to look at things. I practiced this extensively during my time in India. To me, the third alternative was similar to what they call 'Jugaad' in India — innovation. Taking innovative approaches to things that we are faced with. It ultimately became something that was synonymous with me — and it helped us transform the people and the region by exploring alternatives, not letting the traditional way of looking at things get in the way of us achieving our dreams, our goals and our vision.

> Did you know that Switzerland had a civil war? Many people are surprised when they hear this, as Switzerland is famous for being such a beautiful and peaceful country, and you never hear of conflict there. They did have a civil war in 1847, known as the Sonderbund War. It was a conflict between the Catholics and the predominantly Protestant Government. It happened after seven Catholic cantons formed a separate alliance known as the Sonderbund in order to protect their interests against a centralisation of power. The war ended with the defeat of the Sonderbund, in an almost bloodless war. What is even more interesting than the civility and concern for each other expressed by the two sides during the war is the resultant outcome. It is evident that the Swiss looked at how they could do better. And better they did! Rather than one or the other alternative, they came up with a third – a country

> where all their religions, languages, and cultures could flourish, and where their diversity is the source of their strength, even to this day. It trans-formed Switzerland into a federal state.

Can you do better? Are you willing to look for a third way that's beyond 'your way' and 'my way' — a higher way? Not the highway — a HIGHER way, just in case you misread it. In fact, educator and businessman Steven Covey wrote a book called 'The 3rd Alternative: Solving Life's Most Difficult Problems'. If you have not already read it, it is definitely worth doing so. One of the first things I did after listening to Jan was to purchase Covey's book. It gave me a new dimension to my thinking and approach to resolving issues and transformed my leadership to a higher level by opening a whole new world of possibilities to which I was hitherto oblivious.

So, what is standing in your way? What distractions are affecting you? What is holding you back? What can help you and, more importantly, what are you going to do about it? And in my humble words I'll repeat again, "The only person that stands between you and success is YOU."

## What's in it for me?

We have looked at many examples of how things can get in your way and hold you back from realising your dreams, your goals, your vision. Some of the things that will help you deal with what limits your success are: overcoming self-doubt, having a razor-sharp focus, saying "Yes" selectively and saying "No" more often, and finding a third alternative as an effective tool to build successful outcomes. We also looked at the importance of dedicating time to focus on your own self-development, which will become an enabler in your pursuits. And finally, to one of the most common things that stand in our way: excuses.

If making excuses allows you to externalise your failures, then taking responsibility does the opposite. Taking responsibility leads to introspection. You study everything that went wrong and ask yourself, "What could I have done differently" and, "What can I do now to fix it?" When you ask yourself these questions, you feel like you're still in control of your destiny. When you're in control of your destiny, you're motivated to make it the best one possible. And when you're motivated, you work smarter and better. You get what you want.

> James Robertson… has been offered a new car, multiple times, by complete strangers. In fact, a neighbour offered to be his personal chauffeur. Others have offered to pay the insurance bill for whatever new car he ends up with. Why is this generosity coming to him? It could be because The Detroit Free Press wrote an article about him. Why did they do that? Because he walks to work every day. Not that impressive, you say? His commute is 21 miles. James is loyal to his job. When his car broke down and Detroit buses stopped serving his route, he woke up one morning and just started walking. And then he kept doing it. "Tough times don't last. Tough people do." That's what James'

dad told him. It must have stuck. When people heard about his daily marathon commute, people across the country jumped at the opportunity to help someone who was willing to persevere. That's right in line with what researchers at The University of Missouri-Columbia found when they studied the connection between future commitment—the resolve to make something happen—and excuse making. They tested the excuses their subjects would make (or not make) while completing tasks and how that lined up with their resolve to improve. Unsurprisingly, those who made the fewest excuses were the most committed to improving themselves.

The point of the story is not so much about generous strangers as it is about what created them. Who would blame James for giving up in such a dire situation? He could have quit, gone on public assistance, and felt sorry for himself. None of the hardships he endured were his fault. James didn't see it that way, though. That's why strangers are rushing to lend a hand. And it is why people who take responsibility for their own situations—regardless if they deserve the blame for it or not—tend to end up in a better place when the dust settles.

(https://www.riskology.co/making-excuses/)

## So what? What now?

What about you? What stands in the way of achieving your dreams, goals, vision? What excuses do you have?

Put your thinking cap on, do some soul searching, but be true to yourself. Don't try to rationalise; just identify what it really is that distracts you and keeps you from achieving your goals. Like any exercise, the outcomes will only be as good as the input — garbage in, garbage out, as they say. Once you have done this, start identifying what you are going to do about it. Which are the ones that impact you most, which ones will you address as a priority?

We are often quick to blame everything around us, to complain about the speck in our brother's eye, while not seeing the log in ours! It is very important as leaders to have good self-awareness, and to be cognisant of what distractions and impediments we have in our way. Once we know this, we are better able to deal with it. In his summary of Goldsmith's book 'What Got You Here Won't Get You There', James Clear says, "Serious lottery players think success is random. Successful people think success is within their control and thus don't play the lottery. Both mindsets are delusional in their own way, but the successful approach seems to work better overall."[14] And hopefully, you have now identified the most successful approach for yourself.

If you are ready, let's go on a journey that allows you to identify options, challenges you to think, and gives you permission to dream!

---

14 https://bit.ly/3rm8vYf

# CHAPTER 7
# EXPLORE

"Only those who risk going too far can possibly find out how far one can go."

- T.S. Eliot

## How best can you get there?

There was once a young boy who was lazy and unmotivated. He had a very negative mindset and was advised to seek the guidance of Socrates, the wise philosopher. He asked him how to get wisdom, prosperity and success, to which Socrates responded, "Do you really want it? Are you willing to devote yourself to it?" The boy assured him he was, and Socrates told him to meet him by the river the next day. When they met, Socrates ordered the boy to wade into the river and stand there until he was called back. The boy did as he was told, when Socrates walked over to him and pushed him under the water. He kept his head firmly submerged as the boy struggled for air. He finally released the boy, who emerged shocked and gasping for breath. When he regained his composure, Socrates asked him what he most desired when he was underwater. "What I wanted desperately was some air to breathe," he answered. Socrates then told the boy that he could achieve what he desired, be it wisdom, prosperity, success or anything else, as long as he set his mind to it and wanted it as badly as he wanted air when his head was submerged in the water. The boy then understood that intense desire was the key to success.

"I want you to panic, I want you to feel the fear I feel every day. And then I want you to act." Remember these words from Greta Thunberg? Do I really want you to panic at this stage? Do you want to achieve your dreams? Reach your goals? Do you want it as badly as the young boy wanted air? Even if you are not panicking (and there is certainly no need to panic, unless you are lazy like the boy in the story), are you ready to act?

If you are ready to act, then let's examine the options available to you. This is about your definition of how you can get to your dreams, your goals, your vision. There are many techniques out there that will help you do this, so let's explore some of them.

## The more you know, the more you learn

I am certain that you are familiar with 'brainstorming' as a traditional way to generate new ideas. When you brainstorm, you work with whatever ideas come to your mind and let them flow freely. Don't filter the ideas at this stage; the intention is to take note of everything that comes up — there are no bad ideas. You can even use 'word banking' and go through a few rounds of 'word association' to strengthen your ideas. It is commonly perceived that word banking is another term for word association, and that is correct. However, in a word banking session you tend take a more complex approach to the words you come up with. Word banking generally focuses on big groups of terms that represent common trends, themes or topics as opposed to the focus on word pairings common in word association exercises.

Creating word banks can also help break down projects into more manageable parts, similar to a mind map. Then, when your word bank is complete, you can retroactively form connections between the terms you came up with and use those connections to craft ideas that are guaranteed to include all of your most important characteristics.

Mind mapping is another option, if you are the creative type. Mind mapping is a fairly common term nowadays — in fact, many types of software provide automated mind mapping templates so you can better organise your data. Tony Buzan, who popularised mind mapping, argued that the more one knows and learns, the easier it becomes to continue to learn and know even more.

> Adam Sicinski shares a simple introduction to mind mapping:
>
> Mind mapping is a visual information management tool that helps us structure, organize, memorize, arrange, brainstorm and learn information in a highly specialized way. The past 20 years have brought us incredible insights into the human mind and our limitless capacity to think, comprehend and store vast reserves of information. If anything, these studies have highlighted that our capacity to think effectively and quickly is very closely tied to our imagination and our ability to create associations between various information chunks. Mind mapping has come a long way since the early days when Tony Buzan first introduced

> it to the world. It is now on the brink of becoming a mainstream tool used by academics, students, business professionals and many other individuals to manage, organize and reimagine information in a new and highly structured way. These days though, mind mapping isn't just about creating a map. It's instead evolving into a visual information management tool that's transforming the way we think, work, and develop our visual thinking capacity.
>
> (https://blog.iqmatrix.com/how-to-mind-map)

There is also a wishing technique you can follow that encourages you to let your imagination run wild. Dream up the most unattainable, extreme, and impractical solutions you can think of and create a list, compiling what comes to mind. Then, select some of the wishes and explore them in greater detail. This will help you identify which ones are more realistic for you to consider further. What makes them so impossible? How can that idea be scaled down? Don't be surprised to find out that some of your wildest wishes could be viable solutions that you could actually achieve in real life. Remember the BHAGs I shared in Chapter 4?

## What's in it for me?

Your hard work is paying off. You are doing well in your field. But there is something standing between you and the next level of achievement. That something may be just one of your own annoying habits. Perhaps one small flaw — a behaviour you barely even recognise — is the only thing that's keeping you from where you want to be. It may be that the very characteristic that you believe got you where you are — like the drive to win at all costs — is the one that is holding you back. I discussed this idea in Goldsmith's book 'What Got You Here Won't Get You There' in Chapter 2. In fact, I structured an entire two-day workshop around the learnings of this book to prepare and strengthen leaders of leaders for their current and future roles, which I have no doubt truly made an impact on their success as they stepped up to lead others.

As a rising star, one of my trademarks was delivering results. I wasn't even too conscious of this trait until much later in my career because, as you well know, you simply take things in your stride. I remember the very first senior leadership role I took on as director of sales and marketing at the InterContinental Hotel in Colombo, Sri Lanka. When I took on that role mid-year, we were about 10% behind our target for the average room rate we wanted to achieve. My boss at the time threw down the gauntlet by saying that there was no way we could recover to even get close to the target by the end of the year, which meant that we needed to exceed the target for the rest of the year by 20% to make up for the difference. I tackled the challenge head-on. By the end of the year, we hadn't made up the 10% deficit for the year, but we did make up 9%! Thus began a career of delivering exceptional results which became synonymous with my leadership brand.

But as I grew in my leadership and took on more responsibility, it became very evident to me that if I wanted to achieve sustainable results, there was something much more significant than just the numbers. The importance lay not just in the end itself, but in the means to the end — the people. It was quite difficult to make the transition from a 'hard task master' to a 'people person' and I needed to do a lot of reflection and exploration of the path I wanted to chart for my future success. I was very fortunate to have the assistance of a leadership coach, who guided me through the process of transitioning from focusing purely on results to a people-focused approach and gave me a great sounding board that helped reassure me. Though hard at first, I eventually came to enjoy it very much, and actually master it even if I say so myself, and the end result was evident in the success that followed. If you have the right people in the right places, and if you motivate and inspire them, nothing is impossible as I learnt time and time again in my career. In retrospect, Goldsmith's words rang true — what got you here may be the only thing that is keeping you from getting there — and thanks to the guidance of my leadership coach who challenged me to explore options, I was successful in adapting to a new style of leadership, and that actually brought my success to an even higher level. And that's why it is important that we take stock of where we are on our journey vis-à-vis where we want to be, and then exploring those options that are most likely to get us there successfully.

That's a good segue for me to share what is probably the most important leadership lesson I learnt from Jan Smits, as promised in Chapter 6: The importance of focusing on your self-development. Jan championed this cause in the company by leading from the front and ensuring that the focus on developing ourselves and our people was front and centre of everything we did. He was a great proponent of setting aside time from your work schedule to focus specifically on your self-development. He advocated dedicating about 10% of your time, which was quite a bold challenge, but if practiced well could contribute to some great outcomes. Not only did he advocate this but he also led by example. I attribute the focus and practice of my own self-development as one of the biggest contributors to my success and what enabled my amazing leadership journey from such humble beginnings.

At the beginning, you might struggle with this, but the more you practice, the more natural it becomes. And after some time, it becomes your natural way of doing things. Now that you have identified what stands in your way, and have begun to explore options available to you, keep the practice of self-development in mind, as it is a way to realise what you explore. The practice of self-development will help you on your way.

Now it's your time to explore your options. What has worked for you in the past may not be a guarantee of future success. Where you want to go and what you want to achieve may require different skills and behaviours than what you are used to practicing right now. Think about transitioning into a leadership role — before you became a leader, you were only responsible for yourself. My leadership transition took me from managing one person — myself — to leading over 8000 people. The moment you start climbing the leadership ladder, you begin to take responsibility for more and more people. Similarly, what you are setting out to achieve — your dreams, your goals, your vision — may require you to think, act and behave differently. Hence the importance of fully exploring your options on the path to your success.

Arianna Huffington is a well-known name today. She was born in Athens, Greece in 1950, and had a childhood that was impacted by the separation of her parents. During her studies in economics at Cambridge, she stood out for her leadership skills. She subsequently married a US congressman after she moved to the United States. The end of her marriage was a defining moment in her life. Her first attempt to write a book did not receive much encouragement – she was rejected by no less than 26 editors. This made her work even harder to make her project successful, the stress and strain of which caused her to experience fatigue, leading her to collapse.

This made her re-think her life and explore options available to her, which ultimately resulted in her starting a blog in 2005. This blog is what we know now as the Huffington Post, which became a huge success. She is well-known today as one of the most influential persons in the world. This is an inspiring story not only about turning failure into success but is also a great illustration of how successfully exploring your options can bring you success.

## So what? What now?

Now it's your opportunity to explore your options. You can use brainstorming, word banking, mind mapping, wishing or any other method that you are comfortable with, or a combination of them. The idea is to ensure that you explore as many options as possible — who knows, there might be a hidden gem out there that you never thought of before. One thing I learnt when writing this book was that in your first draft you merely keep writing, on and on. Let your creativity flow without any hindrance. Don't interrupt the momentum. No spell check, no editing, that's for later. Consider all the possibilities, even the wildest ones. As kids we all heard the story of Aladdin and the genie, I am sure. What if you were granted one wish; what would it be? Have fun exploring your options. Write down everything that comes up. Keep asking yourself the question 'what else?' continually until you come up with a blank. Make an exhaustive list of all options.

I hope your explorations take you through unknown and unchartered territories, and that you enjoy the exercise. This will hopefully give you some inspiration and motivation to work towards realising your dreams, your goals, your vision. Once you have done this, we can go onto the next interesting step of examining what you discovered.

# Chapter 8
# Validate

"There's a difference between interest and commitment. When you're interested in doing something, you do it only when it's convenient. When you're committed to something, you accept no excuses; only results."

- Ken Blanchard

# What are your commitments and next steps?

This is an excerpt from Napoleon Hill's classic business book, 'Think and Grow Rich' which I feel is especially pertinent:

An uncle of R.U. Darby was caught by the "gold fever" in the gold-rush days and went west to DIG AND GROW RICH. He had never heard that more gold has been mined from the brains of men than has ever been taken from the earth. He staked a claim and went to work with pick and shovel. The going was hard, but his lust for gold was definite.

After weeks of labor, he was rewarded by the discovery of the shining ore. He needed machinery to bring the ore to the surface. Quietly, he covered up the mine, retraced his footsteps to his home in Williamsburg, Maryland, told his relatives and a few neighbors of the "strike." They got together money for the needed machinery, had it shipped. The uncle and Darby went back to work the mine.

The first car of ore was mined, and shipped to a smelter. The returns proved they had one of the richest mines in Colorado!

A few more cars of that ore would clear the debts. Then would come the big killing in profits.

Down went the drills! Up went the hopes of Darby and Uncle! Then something happened! The vein of gold ore disappeared! They had come to the end of the rainbow, and the pot of gold was no longer there! They drilled on, desperately trying to pick up the vein again— all to no avail.

Finally, they decided to QUIT.

They sold the machinery to a junk man for a few hundred dollars, and took the train back home. Some "junk" men are dumb, but not this one! He called in a mining engineer to look at the mine and do a little calculating. The engineer advised that the project had failed, because the owners were not familiar with "fault lines." His calculations showed that the vein would be found JUST THREE FEET FROM WHERE THE DARBYS HAD STOPPED DRILLING! That is exactly where it was found!

The "junk" man took millions of dollars in ore from the mine, because he knew enough to seek expert counsel before giving up.[15]

Why am I retelling this particular story? Because, strangely enough, sometimes it's when people are very close to the finish line that they give up, just three feet away from their gold, because their minds start to play tricks on them. They might get discouraged by people telling them, "It isn't good enough. It's not ready yet. What if people hate it? What if you embarrass yourself? There must be mistakes in it." And

---

15 https://bit.ly/379FIOc

they believe these lies and give up when they are three feet from the gold. I'm telling you this because I do not want it to happen to you.

That is not the only learning for me in this story. There is another key takeaway, and that is the importance of validation — the act of checking the validity or accuracy of something. Imagine if Darby and his uncle in Hill's story took the time or the trouble to validate their assumptions before giving up? You must validate the steps that you identified to get you there — it might save a lot of wasted time and energy as you identify your commitments and actions. If you have been following the process in the previous steps, you should be in a position now to explore various options to realise your dreams, your goals, your vision. Remember the saying, "It is better to be safe than sorry." It is important to validate the options you identified to explore, to ensure you will be on the right path, and that your time, effort and energy will be well-spent, nay, well-invested.

## What's your 'gut' instinct?

As leaders, sometimes we tend to rely on what we call our 'gut' instinct. Some of us by nature are very structured and methodical in our approach to things, others of us may be very instinctive in our approach to things. The former may cringe to see the latter in action, and the latter may think the former is wasting too much time.

Would you believe that someone can predict whether a married couple would be together 15 years later with 90% accuracy, in just 15 minutes? Well, in the 'Love Lab', they can. This is the world's original couples laboratory pioneered by John Gottman, an American psychological researcher and clinician who did extensive work over four decades on divorce prediction and marital stability. But how?

Malcolm Gladwell, well-known best-selling author of 'The Tipping Point', also wrote 'Blink' in which he explains how we are able to arrive at a decision in an instant, made without much thought, or so it seems. He shares that great decision makers are those who are comfortable with what he calls "thin slicing", and not necessarily those who spend a lot of time analysing data, or who are reliant on an enormous amount of information to arrive at their decisions. As he puts it, it's how we "think without thinking."

Many times, I have found that our reluctance to make decisions causes us to ask for more data, which in turn may be merely buying some time before the eventuality. I have many amusing examples when, despite seeking a lot of information or data, we have as a team gone back to the original decision we had in mind! Conversely, I have also been in situations where we stuck to our decisions despite the facts presented to us, which is another subject altogether, but something we should be mindful of because of the adverse impact it can have.

Thin slicing is when our unconscious mind finds patterns in the information we are presented. Since it's our unconscious mind that is at work, it tends to work at speed without us being aware of it. We should not mistake thin slicing with knee-jerk reactions, which are hurried reactions made in response to a situation. We arrive at this 'intuitive' judgment based on thin slicing because we draw on our expertise, knowledge and experience — something that I have put into action often and will be illustrated by an example later on.

In 'Blink', Gladwell aims to show us that our snap judgments can be just as effective and accurate as decisions that are deliberate and well thought out. Further, he wants to convince us that we have power over our intuitive decisions, even though they're unconscious and seem beyond our control.

Gladwell makes a distinction between two processes for arriving at a decision:

1. Conscious Thinking (also known as rational decision making) is when we use logic to weigh the pros and cons of each choice and make a conscious decision. This process is effective, but it takes a long time.

2. Unconscious Thinking (variously known as the adaptive unconscious, intuition, and making snap judgments) is when we make decisions without understanding why, or even realizing we've made them. This process is quick but is sometimes coloured by bias.

We tend to think that conscious thinking is better than unconscious thinking, but both have their time and place.

(https://www.shortform.com/summary/blink-summary-malcolm-gladwell)

# BELIEVE

Why am I introducing this to you now? Throughout my career, I struggled with being comfortable with what I call my 'gut' feel, my instinct. My experience garnered over many decades in a variety of circumstances helped give me a good perspective on things and to 'grow' a great instinct. I had the ability to call something instinctively, and more often than not, would be proven right (thankfully!). I constantly battled with this ability and the need to rationalise it to get the buy-in from the team, who usually preferred a more structured approach to conform to the expectations of the 'norm'. For me, this approach took too much time and consequently made us lose an early-mover advantage or a competitive edge.

One example that comes to mind is when we were considering candidates for a leadership development programme. The moment the subject came up, I shared with the team my choice of a particular person for the programme, as I felt she was ideally suited and that she had what it took to be successful. As we discussed this, there were many questions raised, especially why I made my recommendation — which in fact was based on the only time I met her and had a 15-minute conversation. Sounds rather rash, doesn't it? But sometimes you just know! Of course, the team wanted to follow a more structured approach of inviting applications from a wider audience, and then going through a rigorous assessment process. Since it was a career development programme, I bowed to the pressure, much against my instinct. To cut a long story short, we followed the full process and at the end of it, guess what the outcome was? The candidate I had strongly recommended emerged as the best choice! Subsequently, she went on to complete the programme, and become a very successful general manager. That was an example of how Gladwell's 'Blink' really helped me — it was recommended to me by a dear colleague — as it gave me much more confidence to back my instincts, and I never looked back.

As you begin to validate your options, you have choices too. There is no right or wrong here, it is what you are most comfortable with. If your style is to take a more logical approach, by all means use that. Alternatively, if you are more instinctive, then use that approach. I just want to open your thinking up to the choices you have, to help you with your validation process and to create some awareness in your subconscious about decision making that will hopefully come in handy even at other times.

## What's in it for me?

During my leadership of IHG's South West Asia region there was something that was bothering me, like a stone in my shoe. And every step I took it was a painful reminder of something that we could improve in the region. It all centred around building and maintaining a winning culture, a culture that would rise over and above the day-to-day challenges we faced, a culture that would inspire colleagues to aspire to great things.

In my pursuit of an ideal solution, I did extensive research and came across a tried and tested winning culture model that could be implemented in the organisation. After adapting it to suit the organisation better, I wanted to validate my concept with the leadership team. As a result of the validation process, we were able to take the concept I had identified and made it more relevant by using the behaviours that were a core part of the organisation. And the outcome? The resulting model was so successful that it helped transform the organisation's culture across the region and was instrumental in achieving a top 10 rating in the 'Great Places to Work' ranking across 800+ organisations.[16]

In addition to the programme's success in the region, it was packaged and exported to other regions as a best-practice with much success. And to date, over five years since the introduction of the programme, it has not only survived multiple leadership changes, but continues to be practiced diligently across the region, and thrives as a fundamental part of the culture.

One step I took that changed the programme completely was the step of validation. Had I not done that, I am not so sure if the programme would have been as successful because the link between organisational culture and behaviour would have been missing. Similarly, you need to validate the options you explore before rushing into action, as it might mean the difference between success and failure.

> Article by Karyn Hall PhD on self-validation in Psychology Today:
>
> Validating your thoughts and emotions will help you calm yourself and manage them more effectively. Validating yourself will help you accept and better understand yourself, which leads to a stronger identity and better skills at managing intense emotions. Self-validation helps you find wisdom.

---

16 https://www.greatplacetowork.in/india-best-2018/

Learning to self-validate is not so easy. Notice that mindfulness and self-validation go hand in hand. Being mindful of the thoughts you are having and the feelings you are experiencing is necessary before you can validate that internal experience.

(https://www.psychologytoday.com/us/blog/pieces-mind/201407/self-validation)

In an article on *Huffpost* titled 'Self-Validation: The Unexpected Quality All Effective Leaders Share', the reasons why self-validation is important to leadership is examined:

We all need validation; we need to feel worthy and legitimate. Many of us search for validation in other people. We try to be liked, fit in and be approved of.

For leaders that is quite problematic, because typical leadership traits like following your own path call for autonomous choices.

And autonomy doesn't combine well with needing to be liked.

Leaders are vulnerable when they have to seek validation and appreciation from other people. It will be a constant struggle on a very personal level, withdrawing attention from their actual goals and really relevant challenges. Self-validation is the

> foundation of many of the more visual qualities people attribute to powerful leadership, allowing leaders who have self-validation to be bolder and go further.
>
> (https://bit.ly/378bOKw)
>
> "Much of my work as a psychotherapist is helping people make their words and actions congruent.... Then they have a better chance of others seeing, hearing and validating them because of their consistency. This comes by the person believing in his or her own worth — and not have it depend on what others think," says Connie Ingram, a Florida-based psychologist whose approach to counselling draws from a distinct range of psychological, behavioural and spiritual perspectives.
>
> (https://www.wral.com/commentary-oprah-winfrey-and-the-power-of-validation/17265810/)

## So what? What now?

I expect that expanding your thinking beyond boundaries has helped you come up with a good list of options to explore. Having explored ways to reach your dreams, your goals, your vision, you need to go through a process of validation in order to ensure that you get it right, and you are putting all the learnings thus far to good use as you focus on your actions and commitments thereafter.

Now is the time to narrow the ideas you noted earlier to a few that you would like to consider further. Once you have your list of options to explore, one thing you can do next is SCAMPER; Dani Mansfield explains how to SCAMPER in her article on Brainstorming in a Hubspot blog:

> S.C.A.M.P.E.R. is essentially a process for expanding and improving upon ideas by testing and questioning them from different angles. For each letter of the mnemonic, ask yourself a related question about your project or the problem at hand:
>
> - **S**ubstitute, e.g.: What would happen if we swapped X for Y?
> - **C**ombine, e.g.: What would happen if we combined X and Y?
> - **A**dapt, e.g.: What changes would need to be made to adapt this project to a different context?
> - **M**odify, e.g.: What could we modify to create more value on this project?
> - **P**ut to another use, e.g.: What other uses or applications might this project have?
> - **E**liminate, e.g.: What could we remove from the project to simplify it?
> - **R**everse, e.g.: How could we reorganize this project to make it more effective?
>
> This method forces you to approach your project or problem in unexpected ways. Each question asks you to dig a little deeper into the issue and consider new possibilities.[17]

When you validate your options, it is important that you ensure it is an accurate reflection, because it has a great impact on the actions and next steps you commit to. Be true to yourself, be the authentic you.

---

17 https://blog.hubspot.com/marketing/creative-exercises-better-than-brainstorming

BELIEVE

We are almost there! I hope you are as excited as I am. It is important that you take the time to properly validate your options. Take time to do some self-reflection in addition to the validation before you move onto your final and exciting step of bringing it all to life. So, don't be in a rush, take the time to complete this step in a mindful and meaningful way. Once you are fully satisfied with your validation process, come journey with me to the final step — it seems like we are literally just three feet away!

# CHAPTER 9
# ENABLE

"Impossible is just a big word thrown around by small men who find it easier to live in the world they've been given than to explore the power they have to change it. Impossible is not a fact. It's an opinion. Impossible is not a declaration. It's a dare. Impossible is potential. Impossible is temporary. Impossible is nothing."

- Muhammad Ali

## "Impossible is nothing"

"I don't need arms and legs; I just need Him." This credo helped Nick Vujicic to become one of the most famous motivational speakers, receive an economics degree, get married, have two children and establish the 'Life Without Limbs' ministry in 2005; all without arms and legs. He inherited his strong will from his mother and in his book 'Your Life Without Limits', Nick tells how her words set the tone for a lifetime. "Nicholas," she said, "you need to play with normal children because you are normal. You just have a few bits and pieces missing, that's all." Here's a summary of Nick's story from Life Without Limbs, Nick's website:

> Imagine getting through your busy day without hands or legs. Picture your life without the ability to walk, care for your basic needs, or even embrace those you love. Meet Nicholas Vujicic (pronounced voo-yi-chich). Without any medical explanation or warning, Nick was born in 1982 in Melbourne, Australia, without arms and legs. Three sonograms failed to reveal complications. And yet, the Vujicic family was destined to cope with both the challenge and blessing of raising a son who refused to allow his physical condition to limit his lifestyle.

The early days were difficult. Throughout his childhood, Nick not only dealt with the typical challenges of school and adolescence, but he also struggled with depression and loneliness. Nick constantly wondered why he was different than all the other kids. He questioned the purpose of life, or if he even had a purpose.

According to Nick, the victory over his struggles, as well as his strength and passion for life today, can be credited to his faith in God. His family, friends and the many people he has encountered along the journey have inspired him to carry on.

Since his first speaking engagement at age 19, Nick has travelled around the world. He has shared his story with millions, sometimes in stadiums filled to capacity, speaking to a range of diverse groups such as students, teachers, young people, business professionals and church congregations of all sizes. Today this dynamic young evangelist has accomplished more than most people achieve in a lifetime. He's an author, musician, actor, and his hobbies include fishing, painting and swimming.[18]

The story of Nick Vujicic is truly an inspirational one. With so many odds stacked against him, he could have very well given up, and wallowed in self-pity. Imagine if he did? Think about what he would have given up. I am guessing that the majority of you have a lot more going for you. Are you making the most of what you have? Or are you taking it for granted and not making full use of your potential? Are you going to look back one day with regrets? Or with satisfaction? Are

---

18 https://www.lifewithoutlimbs.org/about-nick/bio/

you giving up on something too easily? Are you stopping your efforts when you might be just three feet away?

## All it takes is to begin, and end

Let me share a secret with you — the most important things you have to do are to begin, and to end; the rest will evolve.

*Aoccdrnig to a rsereearch at Cmabrigde Uinervtisy, it deosn't mttaer in waht oredr the ltteers in a wrod are, the olny iprmoatnt tihng is taht the frist and lsat ltteer be at the rghit pclae. The rset can be a toatl mses and you can sitll raed it wouthit porbelm. Tihs is bcuseae the huamn mnid deos not raed ervey lteter by istlef, but the wrod as a wlohe.*

Got it? I am sure you have. Just in case you haven't, here's how it looks if it is written normally:

*According to a researcher at Cambridge University, it doesn't matter in what order the letters in a word are, the only important thing is that the first and last letter be at the right place. The rest can be a total mess and you can still read it without problem. This is because the human mind does not read every letter by itself but the word as a whole.*

If you get your beginning and ending right, everything else will fall into place. Let's work backwards and start with the end. By now you should have a very clear picture of what your dream, your goal, your vision is. Oprah Winfrey said, "Create the highest grandest vision possible for your life, because you become what you believe!" There is no shame in dreaming big. Don't be shy, go for it!

Now let's look at the beginning. Are you ready? Are you raring to go?

Even though you have a grand vision now (hopefully), start small. Choose one thing to begin with and commit to seeing it through. For those of you who are familiar with cricket, a batsman who makes a big score in a test match is statistically most likely to have started small, then building to the big score, probably facing many balls before he even scores a single run. While you are slow and steady however, it is also important to have quick wins to build up your confidence. Set your sights on something that you can conquer early on, so you can then move on to bigger and better things thereafter. In my cricket analogy, the quick win could be facing 10 balls without getting out, irrespective of the runs you score. As with any goal, make sure you are very specific about what you want to achieve, but also have guardrails around it to keep you honest. Following the SMART principle (Specific, Measurable, Achievable, Realistic and has a Time frame attached to it) is always a useful way to make your goals effective. Then think about what adjustments you need to make it happen. How are you going to find the time? Do you have to give something up? Make a firm commitment and stick to it, come what may. It is important that you don't let yourself down.

## Staying on track

There are a few ways you can keep yourself honest, keep yourself on track. One way is to share your goal with someone else. Someone who will encourage you. Someone who can also 'nudge' you. The moment you externalise a goal, suddenly you will find a lot of energy and enthusiasm is generated. Another rather fun way to do this is to set yourself a consequence. Yes, you heard it right — a consequence for not achieving what you set out to. But it must be something meaningful. On second thought, it should be more than meaningful; it should be painful, something that has a significant impact on you. It has to be difficult to give up.

Let me share a secret with you. I have thought about writing a book for a long time, but it always remained a dream, a goal, a vision, something in my head for many years. I even developed quite a good vision of what the book would be about and what purpose it would serve. Then one day I decided to get serious about it. I felt I needed to have some accountability, so I signed up for a 30-day book writing challenge. Yes, to write a book in 30 days! I did this because I felt it would help keep me on track. But little did I realise the consequences — Joshua Sprague, who was the person providing this framework — asked me to name a consequence if I didn't achieve my goal in the timeframe I committed to, on the very first day of the challenge! I wondered if I had made the wrong choice, but as I had already paid for the course, I decided to give it a go. I set myself a goal to complete a basic draft of the book in 60 days. And guess what? You are reading it right now! Although it took me much longer than 60 days to complete the whole book in the shape and form you see now, I achieved the target I set myself to write the basic draft in 60 days. And do you want to know what the consequence I set for myself was? I would refrain from using the internet for three days — imagine what life would have been like? That fear made me focus on achieving my goal, come what may.

So, are you ready now? Are you raring to go?

### "I'll play"

Sweet 16 is a recurring theme in this book; from Richard Branson's early pursuits to the amazing global movement started by Greta Thunberg. Here's another inspiring story of a 16-year-old boy, this time a cricketer. Those of you who are familiar with cricket would no doubt know of Sachin Tendulkar who is widely regarded as one of the greatest batsmen in the history of cricket. They say that with two words, "Main khelega" (I'll play) his talent transformed him into a genius on the last day of the last test match between India and Pakistan in Sialkot, Pakistan in December 1989. With India in a bad way at four wickets down for just 38 runs, Sachin walked on to bat in his first test series as a young 16 year old. He faced a fierce pace bowling attack comprising three of the greats – Wasim Akram, Waqar Younis and Imran Khan – and was welcomed by a bouncer from Waqar that fractured his nose, blood spurting everywhere. He was advised to leave the ground immediately, and the physio was about to call a stretcher. Seemingly annoyed at the suggestion, Sachin brushed them aside saying, "Main khelega" and continued. He hit the next ball for a boundary and went on to score a match-saving 57 runs. Navjot Singh Sidhu, who batted with Sachin that day, says a star was born with the words "I'll play".

> Where some of the experienced batsmen had failed, Sachin stood tall. What separates the champions from others is not just talent, it's the sheer determination to succeed, no matter what. It's the strength to fight on, especially when things are not going your way.

## What's in it for me?

Jack Welch, former CEO of General Electric, once said that what determines your destiny is not the hand you're dealt; it's how you play the hand. And the best way to play your hand is to face reality—see the world the way it is—and act accordingly. Remember 'Be Real'? Remember the orphan who accidently ventured into a career in hospitality? What if….

Are you determined to succeed, no matter what? There is only one person, and one person only, who is crucial in enabling your success; and that person is you!

## So what? What now?

The headline of an interview with Jack Welch titled 'Speed, Simplicity, Self-Confidence' caught my attention. He said that "Good business leaders create a vision, articulate the vision, passionately own the vision, and relentlessly drive it to completion."[19] And as you reflect on enabling your dreams, your goals, your vision, I feel these very things can ring true. We live in more uncertain times than we've ever experienced before. Sitting back and waiting for the air to clear,

---

19  https://bit.ly/3mGJYJS

for things to get better, aren't going to make you a winner. You need to act, and you need to act with speed and agility. Similarly, when it comes to enabling your plan to realise your dreams, your goals, your vision, don't put it off. Don't wait for tomorrow — tomorrow may never come, as the saying goes. Start today, start now.

We all know the KISS principle — not the physical one — but the principle it stands for: Keep it Simple Smart (which is my version). Don't over complicate things. Take baby steps. But take them consistently and regularly. There is a saying that tiny drops make a mighty ocean. Keeping things simple will help you to secure some quick wins, which will boost your confidence. With greater confidence you will be more courageous and not be afraid to challenge the status quo, push the boundaries and go on to achieve bigger and better things. You can adopt this very simple principle to enable your dreams, your goals, your vision, and unleash the power of your true potential — remember, *Speed, Simplicity, Self-Confidence.*

What was your new year's resolution, if you had one? I am not sure what time of the year you are reading this, but what success are you likely to have in fulfilling your new year's resolution? According to *Forbes* magazine, the statistics on how many people actually follow through and accomplish their resolutions are rather grim. Less than 25% of people actually stay committed after just 30 days, and only 8% accomplish them. *Forbes* encourages its readers to set goals instead of resolutions. Why goals you may ask? Their answer: "That's simple — because goals are specific, whereas resolutions tend to be broad and vague. Goals are much more actionable, which is what makes them more effective."[20]

How are you feeling right now? Do you feel like you believe, that you are now enabled to make it happen, to make the impossible possible?

What are you waiting for? As Nike says, "Just Do It!"

---

[20] https://bit.ly/37XlOW7

# CHAPTER 10
# SAY YES TO NO

"In the beginner's mind there are many possibilities, in the expert, there are few."

- Suzuki Roshi

# FROM FIVE DOLLARS TO A BILLION DOLLARS. IF I CAN, WHY CAN'T YOU?

Growing up, Roger Federer took a keen interest in sports. At the age of eight he was playing both soccer and tennis. He became one of the top three junior tennis players in Switzerland by the time he was 11. At the age of 12 Federer made a crucial and probably the most important decision of his life. He had to say "No" to all other sports in order to focus his efforts on tennis, as he felt that he excelled more naturally at that sport. By the age of 14 Federer was fully focused on tennis, playing in a few tournaments every month. He often looked to other great players, including Boris Becker and Stefan Edberg, to improve his game further.

Roger Federer is my most admired sportsman of all time — despite my upbringing in cricket-mad countries and my love for the sport and some of the greatest players that ever played the game. I hold cricketers like Kumar Sangakkara, Sachin Tendulkar, M S Dhoni and Mahela Jayawardena in very high esteem, not because of their great talent and achievements in the game, but because of their amazing sporting personalities; much like Federer.

## BELIEVE

I must confess though that my love for Federer was likely sparked by the greatest love of my life — my wife Renu — and her ardent admiration for him. He is widely recognised as one of the greatest tennis players in history and to-date, he has won 20 Grand Slam men's singles championships and holds the record for winning the most. To attain that level of achievement, he had a tough choice to make, and so do you. Just imagine if he didn't have the courage to make the tough call and say "No" and instead continued with all the sports he was involved in — would he have been transformed into the champion he is today? Perhaps with his natural talent he would have excelled at all of them. However, it is difficult to believe that he would have reached the pinnacle of success had he not said "No" to the other sports.

This example from Roger Federer is an important but tough lesson I learnt myself. I often faced crossroads when I eagerly tried to take on too many projects and responsibilities. A bad habit that developed was that in my over-enthusiasm, I would say "Yes", then figure out the details later, often to my own detriment. Learning to say "No" was difficult and very uncomfortable at the beginning. But once I understood and identified why I needed to say "No", it made it a lot easier. It helped that many of my team members would often give me gentle reminders that we were human too! I particularly appreciated that they were never shy to challenge my thinking, which helped me not to stray from the straight and narrow path of focus — which paid off in the long run. Next time, before you say "Yes" without giving it much thought, think about the impact it could have had on Federer.

The quote at the beginning of this chapter is from Suzuki Roshi who is credited with founding the first Zen Buddhist monastery outside of Asia and for popularising Zen Buddhism in the United States. His intention was not to say that we shouldn't gather skill, knowledge, and expertise. All he was doing was pointing out the fact that the mind has a tendency to compare what's happening to what could, should, or would be happening — and that comparison holds us back. I debated about including this quotation in the book as I struggled quite a bit with it. In the end I decided to include it because to me it revealed some great truths, even though I find it quite polarising. I thought that going through a similar mental struggle might also challenge and expand your thinking. I quite like the concept of a beginner's mindset, a state of mind which is judgment-free, open, curious, available, and present. Maybe controversially, I also take great value from the latter part of the statement that relates to the expert's mind having few possibilities. I look at this in conjunction with Federer making the decision to say "No" so he could focus on his chosen field, and I derive a very powerful outcome: Focusing on fewer possibilities has an impact on helping you become an expert in your chosen field.

Remember the learnings from Jan I shared in Chapter 6? Do you want to be a Jack of all trades and master of none? If not, then what are you going to stop doing? What are you going to say "No" to?

> Each time the New Year rolls around and I sit down to do my annual resolutions, I reflect back to a lesson taught me by a remarkable teacher. In my mid-20s, I took a course on creativity and innovation from Rochelle Myers and Michael Ray at the Stanford

Graduate School of Business, and I kept in touch with them after I graduated.

One day, Rochelle pointed to my ferocious work pace and said, "I notice, Jim, that you are a rather undisciplined person."

I was stunned and confused. After all, I was the type of person who carefully laid out my BHAGs (big hairy audacious goals), top three objectives and priority activities at the start of each New Year. I prided myself on the ability to work relentlessly toward those objectives, applying the energy I'd inherited from my prairie-stock grandmother.

"Your genetic energy level enables your lack of discipline," Rochelle continued. "Instead of leading a disciplined life, you lead a busy life."

She then gave me what I came to call the 20-10 assignment. It goes like this: Suppose you woke up tomorrow and received two phone calls. The first phone call tells you that you have inherited $20 million, no strings attached. The second tells you that you have an incurable and terminal disease, and you have no more than 10 years to live. What would you do differently, and, in particular, what would you stop doing?

That assignment became a turning point in my life, and the "stop doing" list became an enduring cornerstone of my annual New Year resolutions—a mechanism for disciplined thought about how to allocate the most precious of all resources: time.

Rochelle's challenge forced me to see that I'd been plenty energetic, but on the wrong things. Indeed, I was on entirely the wrong path. After graduate school, I'd taken a job at Hewlett-Packard. I loved the company, but hated the job. Rochelle's assignment helped me see I was cut out to be a professor, a researcher, a teacher—not a businessman—and I needed to make a right-angle turn. I had to stop doing my career, so that I could find my real work. I quit HP, migrated to the Stanford Business School faculty and eventually became—with some remarkable good luck along the way—a self-employed professor, happily toiling away on my research and writing.

(https://www.jimcollins.com/article_topics/articles/best-new-years.html)

This is an excerpt from an interesting article by Jim Collins published in USA Today titled 'The Best New Year's Resolution? A 'Stop Doing' List' that aptly illustrates the importance of saying "No". What a powerful story. Just imagine if Jim Collins did not say "No" and continued as he was – we probably would not have been privileged to benefit from his research and writings, which has had a massive impact on my success.

In his book 'Good to Great', Collins shares the 'Hedgehog concept' that will help you to identify what you should prioritise and focus on:

1. What you are deeply passionate about
2. What you can be the best in the world at
3. What drives your economic engine[21]

This concept can be applied to your life and those fortunate enough to find or create a practical intersection of the three circles have the basis for achieving success both in their life and leadership journey.

Marshall Goldsmith, whom I mentioned earlier, shared one of the greatest lessons he learnt from Peter Drucker, known as the world's authority on management. Drucker said, "We spend a lot of time helping leaders learn what to do. We do not spend enough time teaching leaders what to stop. Half of the leaders I have met don't need to learn what to do. They need to learn what to stop."[22] In Goldsmith's book 'What Got You Here Won't Get You There', which I referenced earlier, he shares 20 bad habits of leaders. And he says the one habit that takes precedence over all others is the need to win at all costs and in all situations! (If you would like to access the list, visit his website marshallgoldsmith.com, and you can download the list for free.)

I also love the concept of the 'Golden Circle':

According to Simon Sinek, most companies have no idea why customers choose their products. Successful companies, however, let their customer approach driven by three questions that make up the Golden Circle; Why, How and What.

---

21 Collins, J.C. (2001). *Good to Great: Why Some Companies Make the Leap... and Others Don't.* HarperCollins, p. 118.
22 Goldsmith, M. (2007). *What Got You Here Won't Get You There.* Hyperion, p. 35.

The WHAT ring of the Golden Circle represents the products or services a company sells.

The HOW is an explanation of what the company does.

The WHY is about what a company believes in and their values.

The underlying premise is that consumers do not buy products because of WHAT companies do, but because of WHY they do it.

Most companies work from the outside in. They start with the WHAT question describing what they offer. When articulating their Unique Selling Point (USP), these companies can only articulate the technical benefits of their offer and how their offer differentiates from the competition.

Inspired and influential companies communicate from the inside out rather than outside in. So instead of communicating WHAT they do and HOW they make it, they communicate their vision to their customer and WHY they exist as a company.[23]

I constantly challenge myself to go back to my purpose, to my own 'why', not only as a reminder as to why I do what I do, but also as a litmus test to guide me in my decisions. I find this to be an especially effective way to evaluate key decisions. Next time you find yourself faced with a dilemma, revisiting your 'why' may prove to be beneficial.

So, as you set out to unleash your true potential, a little bit of self-examination of your core to explore why you do things may be apt. Sinek also wrote the book 'Find Your Why', which is helpful if you

---

23  https://www.innovationcanvas.ktn-uk.org/resources/golden-circle

want to explore and establish your why, to help you get more out of life, more out of yourself, and more out of your work. Understanding your why will definitely help you make the right choices in your life and work and give you the confidence to say "No" when you need to. The learnings from these 'giants' in their fields gives you something to think about and provides an ideal confluence of ideas to set you up for success as you start unleashing your true potential.

Let me share the reason why I do what I do: It is my passion *to make the world a better place by striving to be a better person, and an inspiration to others.* I strive to be a better person to those I love and care about, to my neighbour (in the biblical meaning of the word) and to those in need.

I have been blessed with so many things in my life that I am truly grateful for: the love of an amazing family who have always been there for me, no matter what; the guidance of some great leaders who gave me opportunities and second chances; exceptional teams and awesome people who supported me, without whom nothing would have been possible; all of which contributed to the amazing career I enjoyed and the life I now cherish. One word defines all this for me, and that word is BELIEVE. I believed in God. I believed in myself, and my ability to unleash my true potential; and so did my family, my leaders and the many people I was lucky to work with — they all believed in me. And it proved beyond doubt what the power of belief can do — it took me from five dollars to a billion dollars, amongst other things. See what it holds for you by unlocking your true potential.

I hope what I have shared throughout this book will serve as an inspiration to you to believe in yourself and unlock your true potential, so that it helps make your life and your career a little bit better. To borrow a phrase from Roger Federer, "Being No. 1 was a kid's dream for me. Chasing it made me who I am today."

Remember, the only person that stands between you and success is YOU!

Go on, BELIEVE and unlock your true potential!

# Epilogue

"The only person that stands between you and success is YOU"

- Shantha de Silva

In the earlier chapters I promised to share two sequels to stories that I shared with you, and that time is now. I hope it will help to further reinforce the outcomes from some of the steps we have explored, and the benefits if done well.

When my boss asked me the question about when I was going to win an award at my very first General Managers Leadership Conference, it ignited a fire in me, a passion to excel and make him proud. He had, just a few months earlier, entrusted me with the responsibilities of being a GM for the first time. Additionally, it was in the key city of Singapore and I wanted to pay back the faith he placed in me. Well, this story has a happy ending. As a GM, the hotels I managed won several awards over the years, building quite a reputation for me too. In addition, I was honoured to receive many awards and recognition, culminating in the ultimate recognition of the CEO's Internal Flame award.

Then to our adventures in India. We started a journey to make India #1 for IHG, and IHG #1 for India. I am proud to say that we pretty much achieved those objectives. At the outset, India was one of the underperforming regions in IHG. From there we went on to have an amazing track record to become one of the best performing regions in IHG for three years in a row. We went from learning from other regions to leading other regions in sharing best practices. Externally, in a period of over three years, we managed to double our portfolio of hotels in India and signed possibly the largest hotel portfolio conversion deal in the history of hospitality in India! Needless to say, I had the support of an incredible team that made it all possible.

In retrospect, all this would not have been possible had I not believed, and more importantly if the team did not believe. Each of the steps in the BELIEVE model has an impact and influence on how we unlock and realise our true potential. Depending on our individual circumstances some may apply more than others. At various times we might have to dial up and dial down some of the elements. Like the engine of a race car, we need to fine-tune it to bring out the best outcomes for ourselves.

My hope is that not only will you reap the benefits as much as I did, but that you will also share your story and success with others so as to inspire them!

## WANT TO IMPROVE YOUR LEADERSHIP?

To be a great leader you have to use every opportunity to improve, to progress, to get a little bit closer to your goal. It might seem like a lot of effort — and with a busy schedule, next to impossible to achieve. The good news is that the more you accomplish, the more motivated you will be, and more you will strive for even greater heights.

## BELIEVE

Whether you are an emerging leader, a leader transitioning into a new role or a successful leader at the peak of your career, the BELIEVE model provides you with seven practical steps that will guide and support you in unlocking your true potential and in achieving your dreams, your goals, your vision.

*The only person that stands between you and success is YOU.*

# CHANGING LEADERS, ONE LEADER AT A TIME

Drawing on his vast experience and expertise, Shantha helps leaders to consider different perspectives, question assumptions, and practise new ways of thinking by providing them with the strength and motivation to challenge themselves and their teams to reach greater heights. Through executive coaching and leadership mentoring he helps leaders balance their personal and professional goals, so they can enjoy healthy, balanced lifestyles.

## Executive coaching

Coaching inspires leaders to try new things, discover new opportunities and achieve greater successes that sometimes they never imagined possible. Through executive coaching Shantha helps you to unlock and realise your true potential; to focus on the shift in mindset from being engrossed in the day-to-day to taking a clearer, more strategic view of what is going on to become a better leader.

## Leadership mentoring

We know that directing people 'to do' does not produce great results as compared to inspiring people so they 'want to do'. Over time we have discovered the reason why, but knowing 'why' is not what creates success; it is the 'how' that does. Mentoring is the 'how', inspiring people to want to reach greater heights.

Shantha helps leaders who are seeking personal and professional development through leadership mentoring to inspire, empower and support them, helping leaders set important goals and develop the skills to reach them.

To find out more visit: www.shanthadesilva.com

# About Shantha

Shantha is a senior leader with over 35 years of global experience and expertise leading businesses across South East and South West Asia, the South Pacific and Australasia, responsible for an annual turnover of nearly 1 billion AUD and over 8000 associates. He has also served on several boards and chaired a social initiative for the Government of Singapore.

He has an outstanding reputation for challenging the status quo and transforming businesses across those regions to achieve top performer status. He conceptualised and implemented a company-wide culture programme that championed the value of team members, evolving into a way of life across the businesses, resulting in a national top 10 rating in employer branding across a platform of 800+ organisations.

He is an inspirational mentor and coach, growing talent and helping leaders unlock their true potential, guiding them to achieve successful outcomes in their careers and transition into senior leadership roles.

He is passionate about those differently abled, leading a national initiative, initiating a national recognition programme and developing training centres to enhance the job readiness of those differently abled.

He overcame many a challenge in life, having lost his parents while still in his teens, to build a very successful career through passion, determination and belief. He is a proud father of two sons, a loving husband, and is passionate about paying it forward to make the world a better place by striving to be a better person, and an inspiration to others.

www.ingramcontent.com/pod-product-compliance
Lightning Source LLC
Chambersburg PA
CBHW050314010526
44107CB00055B/2241